In the Cause of English Lace

Catherine C. Channer, c. 1899.

In the Cause of English Lace

The Life and Work of
Catherine C. Channer 1874-1949

by Anne Buck

incorporating

Lace-making in the Midlands, Past and Present

by Catherine C. Channer and
Margaret E. Roberts

RUTH BEAN
CARLTON · BEDFORD
1991

Lace-making in the Midlands, Past and Present, by C. C. Channer
and M. E. Roberts was originally published by Methuen & Co.,
London, 1900. This edition is published by
Ruth Bean Publishers, Carlton, Bedford MK43 7LP, England.

ISBN 0 903585 26 x

Designed by Alan Bultitude at the
September Press, Irchester, Northants NN9 7AB.

Printed in Great Britain
by Jolly & Barber Ltd, Rugby.

Cover photograph: *Edward Turner and his wife Cassandra*, c.
1745, by Allan Ramsay, on loan from the Page-Turner Estate to
The National Trust, Canons Ashby, Northamptonshire. Their
younger son, John, married Elizabeth Dryden and inherited
Canons Ashby, becoming Sir John Turner Dryden in 1795. His
great-niece, Alice Dryden of Canons Ashby, was an active
supporter of the work of the Lace Associations.

CONTENTS

LIST OF ILLUSTRATIONS

FIGURES

7

ACKNOWLEDGEMENTS

We are indebted to Mrs Sandra King, who kindly lent us her rare copy of *Lace-making in the Midlands*. The illustrations were photographed from a copy in Luton Museum. We are grateful to the Curator for allowing us to use this, also to the Curators of Northampton Museum and the Cecil Higgins Art Gallery, Bedford, for permission to photograph items in their collections, and to the Administrator, Canons Ashby, for permission to photograph the portrait of Edward and Cassandra Turner. Miss K. Richards, Mrs E. Routley and Miss B.J. Savage kindly allowed us to use photographs from their private collections. Our thanks go to Miss J. Hodgkinson of Northampton Museum; to Miss A. George, then of the Cecil Higgins Art Gallery, Bedford; to Miss J. Draper of Luton Museum, and to Mrs V. Bullard and Mrs E. Arnold for their help. Plates 7, 11, and 12 are reproduced by permission of the Northamptonshire Record Office. We would also like to acknowledge the contribution of Mrs Patricia Bury to the pattern for the lace mat (*Plate 3*) published separately as a supplement.

NOTE ON THE REPRINT EDITION OF
Lace-making in the Midlands

The text of *Lace-making in the Midlands* is reproduced verbatim, including contemporary spelling and punctuation. In her letter from India (p. 13) Miss Channer apologises for mistakes in the book but does not specify errata. Even obvious examples, such as *Mariote* (p. 49), *quilted* (p. 57) and *rôle* (p. 66), have not been corrected but should probably read Marriott, quilled and roll, respectively.

The Contents and List of Illustrations from the original work have been incorporated into the overall Contents and List of Illustrations at the beginning of this book. The original text did not allocate figure references for illustrations on facing pages, which have now been added within square brackets. Some illustrations have been enlarged for greater clarity. Editor's notes are given as footnotes or (as dates) in square brackets within the text.

Page numbering in this book runs consecutively throughout, including the reprint section in the middle, and all page references relate to this edition rather than to the original.

FOREWORD

LACEMAKERS of today know Catherine C. Channer through her book, *Practical Lacemaking*, first published in 1928 and re-issued, with the revival of lacemaking, in 1953. A few who valued and admired this work may have been fortunate enough to discover a rare, second-hand, copy of a book she wrote thirty years earlier with Margaret E. Roberts, *Lace-making in the Midlands*, which has been out of print for many years.

In response to the interest of many lacemakers of the present generation this early work is now being reprinted here.

Miss Channer spent all her life working in and for lace. It seemed time that some one who had personal recollection of her should take up the story of the lace industry in Bedfordshire, Buckinghamshire and Northamptonshire from the point where she and Miss Roberts left it in 1900 and record her achievement and contribution to English lacemaking during the next forty years.

CATHERINE C. CHANNER
1874-1949

LACEWOMAN AND TEACHER

By Anne Buck

Lace-making in the Midlands Past and Present is reprinted here for the first time since it was first published in 1900. Its authors, C. C. Channer and M. E. Roberts, were both daughters of Northamptonshire clergymen who lived in the neighbouring villages of Ravensthorpe and Spratton. Miss Channer, who was born in Devon in 1874, was the daughter of Edgar Campbell Channer who, after holding livings in London and Essex, moved to Northamptonshire, first to Desborough in 1887 and then to Ravensthorpe in 1894.

Miss Roberts was Margaret Emily Roberts daughter of the vicar of Spratton and born there in 1865. So both of them had grown up amongst Northamptonshire lacemakers. Miss Roberts's mother, Georgina Roberts, had for some years helped lacemakers, unable to sell their lace as dealers went out of business, by organising its sale amongst her friends. An accomplished lacemaker herself, she also organised classes for girls over eleven years of age when the Education Act of 1870 led to the end of the lace schools. Many years later, in 1926, she published a book of the lace patterns worked in and around Spratton. Margaret Roberts studied design under Mr Knight at the Technical School in Northampton and taught herself to apply this training to the design of new lace patterns. One of her designs, for a fan, appears in the book (*Fig. 16*). Fans with leaves of lace were fashionable dress accessories between 1870 and 1910; this lace leaf shows the influence of her training in contemporary design.

Miss Channer seems to have had no formal training in lacemaking or design. There is no mention of it in the book and, during the years I knew her, from 1938, she never spoke of any, although I

11

learnt that her sister Frances was an embroiderer, trained at the Royal School of Needlework which had been established in 1872. Later in the 1930s Miss Channer taught embroidery as well as lacemaking in her classes at Bedford. It seems most likely that she taught herself lacemaking under the guidance of Mrs Roberts and learnt much from the older generation of lacemakers. By the 1890s she was herself teaching lacemaking in Spratton 'where real Valenciennes was taught' (p. 78) and at East Haddon about two miles south of Ravensthorpe. We get an early glimpse of her 'travelling on bicycle or on horseback from one village to another holding more than one class a day in villages three or four miles apart' (p. 78).

Growing up in this district she had seen the industry decline around her, bringing added hardship to village life. She became aware that the decline was not due entirely to the competition of machine-made lace. As earnings from it fell lacemaking lost its status as an employment, 'We have many proofs of what was done to bring contempt upon the lace industry.... Farmers' wives still speak contemptuously of lacemaking and twelve or fourteen years ago few of the landowners cared anything for the trade' (p. 65). Lacemakers themselves thought that earnings from lace helped to depress agricultural wages. The older workers whose memories went back to the 1840s and 1850s said to this young enthusiast, 'I always loved my pillow'; the middle-aged and younger women said 'I hate it' (p. 64) and turned to domestic service.

Miss Channer studied and discussed with the older women the patterns they had worked in the 1840s and 1850s and learnt from them the traditional ways of working. She always spoke of them with the respect of a fellow craftswoman and the rest of her life was spent reviving, developing and passing on their skills. Her knowledge based on long study and constant practice covered all types of lace. What she wrote of Mrs Roberts, 'there was no lace she did not understand' was also true of Miss Channer. That she was already a skilled worker in her early twenties can be seen from the lace shown in Figure 15.

12

In 1899, just before the book was published, Miss Roberts married Henry Chubb, who had been curate at Spratton 1891-1894 and Miss Channer set out for India. She wrote a letter to the *Northampton Herald* (10 December 1900) from India, where she was living with her brother, a forest officer, in a series of forest bungalows, thanking them for their 'very kind review of my little book'. She and Miss Roberts had been vexed at the delay in publishing it because its aim had been to describe things 'exactly as they were' and she apologises for some errors in it due to the loss of proofs between India and England. She also revealed that Miss Roberts, 'no longer Miss Roberts' had, like her, left North-amptonshire. Lacemaking she found was a splendid occupation for jungle life, 'When we move to another bungalow or pitch our tents in a fresh spot my pillow is rolled in a hold-all and strapped to the back of a camel or dumped in a bullock cart with our other belongings. The luggage goes in the night and when we arrive next day after our pleasant early morning ride along beautiful forest roads there is a pillow and lace-horse set ready for me by attentive turbanned servants.' She remained in India until 1909 and from 1905 taught lacemaking at a school for home industries run by the Scots Mission at Kalimpong.

When she returned to England she worked for a time with the Midland Lace Association (*Pl. 1*). The last two chapters of the book give an account of the early years of the Association and her involvement with it and its problems in the 1890s, before she left for India. The Association must have welcomed her help on her return. She worked first from Spratton, collecting lace from village workers and teaching in village classes (*Pl. 2*) and then at the Association's headquarters in Northampton, from 1912 to 1914, before setting up her own lace business and school at 10a St Giles Square, Northampton, buying and selling lace, supplying lacemaking patterns, equipment and materials and holding classes in lacemaking.

She collected drafts and parchment patterns left by dealers as lace businesses closed with the declining trade. In an article, *Local Lacemaking*, in the *Northampton Independent* (July 1914) she wrote,

13

The following are two recent Testimonials :—

I have great pleasure in testifying to Miss Channer's great ability as a teacher and maker of pillow lace.

Many years ago she held classes in Spratton for teaching Valenciennes lace. Since then she has perfected herself in all the various kinds, and there is not one the mysteries of which she could not now unravel.

As a teacher she is most patient and painstaking, never sparing herself any trouble in order to perfect her pupils in the art.

Italian lace with its beautiful " fillings " she is past master of, but whatever lace a pupil desires to learn she is fully competent to teach. She is also very clever in pricking and designing lace patterns, and has conquered the hitherto (to amateurs) very difficult problem of drafting grounds after the old Bucks. style.

In lace mending and cleaning she is also an expert, as also in making up lace-trimmed articles of all kinds.

(Signed) G. M. ROBERTS,
Spratton, Northampton.

Miss C. C. Channer was in charge of our Lace School at Kalimpong for four years between 1905 and 1909, and I have the greatest pleasure in testifying to her excellent abilities as a teacher of lace-making.

Her intimate knowledge of so many varieties of lace-making gives her an exceptional position as a teacher. She teaches thoroughly all the different kinds of pillow lace made on the Continent of Europe, including Brussels, Italian, etc., and she also teaches the kinds made in Buckinghamshire and Honiton in England. She placed our school in the front rank, and has been the means of initiating and bringing to great perfection this beautiful industry among the women of our district, and through the teachers whom she has trained a beginning has been made in other parts of the province of Bengal. Miss Channer is an indefatigable worker, and commands thorough discipline among her pupils, whilst she is animated by the highest motives in her work.

It is on account of health that she has had to return to England, but we are glad that she is still to be associated with us in making designs, advising, and in other ways that will be helpful.

I can recommend Miss Channer to any such similar work with complete confidence.

(Signed) K. GRAHAM,
Lady Superintendent of the Kalimpong
Home Industries, Bengal, India.

PLATE 1. Printed leaflet issued by Miss Channer on her return from India when she established herself as a teacher and dealer in lace at Spratton, c. 1910. One testimonial is from Mrs G. M. Roberts, a founder member of the Midland Lace Association and mother of Miss M. E. Roberts, co-author with Miss Channer of *Lace-making in the Midlands*. The other testimonial records her work in India. (*Mrs E. Routley*)

'There is still a little trade and it has revived and strengthened during the last four or five years. There are still a few lacebuyers in Northampton and more in such places as Olney and Stony Stratford, and still a few, a very few, people who can prick point ground parchments properly. This pricking is so far a lost art that it took me years of study and enquiry of all sorts of people to discover, first a really practicable easy modern method of drafting for point ground parchments, and then (out of curiosity) the exact methods of prickers 50 years ago.' Patient working out of a

15

PLATE 2. The house at Spratton, Northants, where Miss Channer had her lace school and sold lace, 1910-2. (*Miss B. J. Savage*)

problem and lively curiosity were amongst her endearing and enduring qualities.

The Lace School, Northampton survived the war years 1914-18 and Miss Channer continued to work from there during the 1920s. She also took classes in lacemaking at the School of Arts and Crafts which had been established in 1907. In 1925 she started classes in lacemaking with the Bedford Technical Institute, a newly established organisation for adult education with evening and Saturday afternoon classes in Bedford schools. Then early in the 1930s she moved her headquarters from Northampton to 3a Broadway, Bedford. In 1928 she had published her second book, *Practical Lacemaking*, a book of instructions and patterns for point ground lace, as a textbook for her students. Very few books of practical instruction were then available. In it she describes the method she had worked out for pricking the ground for new patterns. The frontispiece shows one of her own designs, a lace mat, 'worked by a student at Bedford Technical Institute'. In a later edition of *Practical Lacemaking* (edited by M. Waller, 1953) the student is identified as Mrs Dixon of Clapham. The lace is now in the Cecil Higgins Art Gallery, Bedford (*Pl. 3*).

I first met Miss Channer when she came to give a demonstration of lacemaking at Luton Museum for the opening of a new room of rural industries. I had just begun to work there. She sat at her pillow with its hundred or more bobbins, talking to the people clustered round her as her hands moved, adding stitch by stitch to a broad point ground lace of traditional pattern, a quiet woman, white haired with bright humorous eyes behind gold-rimmed spectacles. The museum had collected and was continuing to collect material to record and illustrate the lace industry. Miss Channer had been much in advance of her time in making a plea for a lace museum at Northampton in 1900 (p. 84) and she readily co-operated with Luton Museum. Many examples of lace, parchment patterns, bobbins and bobbin winders, pillow horses and candle stools which families of lacemakers were abandoning came to the museum at her suggestion. She helped its work in many ways, not only by directing gifts to it, but in identifying and assessing lace offered

17

and making available all her experience in the local industry and her wide knowledge of European lacemaking.

Soon after that meeting in 1938 museum work everywhere was interrupted first by the threat of war in 1938 and then by its outbreak in 1939. This also brought the classes of the Bedford Technical Institute to an end and Miss Channer, now sixty-five years old, gave up her business in Bedford and moved to Clapham to a house of four flats recently built by the Soroptimists. She offered the museum a choice of material still remaining in the shop in Bedford which she had collected and kept for her own use and interest. The lacemaking collection at the museum had become my responsibility and study and I went to Bedford to make this choice. Her generous gift included a large selection of pattern drafts which she had acquired over many years often from dealers as they went out of business. These now form a unique archive for lacemakers at Luton Museum.

I now knew that to understand lacemaking and to be able to interpret it and all the objects connected with it I had to learn how to make lace. I asked Miss Channer if she would give me a few private lessons, as there were then no classes available, to support my efforts to learn from *Practical Lacemaking*. She agreed and I made several journeys at irregular intervals from Luton to Clapham, by train to Bedford, walking to Clapham but usually managing to catch a bus back to Bedford after two hours of teaching and talk. I carried my pillow with me set up first with a fan pattern, the one chosen for beginners in her book, then with slightly more difficult edgings and borders, but always point ground work. I never became a good lacemaker but I acquired a lasting respect for the skill of the workers who had made the lace I handled in the museum.

Miss Channer interpreted the old drafts for me, pointing out that a line drawn outside a pricked shape meant the use of a gimp thread, a line drawn inside simply gave the outline of the shape; that straight lines, double or single, meant single legs or bars, holes pricked close to them mean picots, and a single hole a point of crossing. Square plaits were shown by dots, leaf plaits by an oval

18

mark. She pointed out that the lacemakers of the Midlands generally used four pairs of bobbins for the footside of their lace whereas Lille lace which the East Midlands lace most closely resembles, shows only three; that in torchon they filled in the squares which elsewhere were worked with an open centre. She was, though, always cautious about identifying a place of origin from design or technique alone. After all she herself had made Italian style lace in Northamptonshire (*Fig. 15*) and had taught Valenciennes lace to lacemakers at Spratton. A characteristic comment as she identified and assessed lace for Luton Museum would be, 'old type with fine thread and thick, soft gimp, common in South Northamptonshire'; this was as far as she would go.

She showed me how important the actual placing of pins was, how to put them in so that the lace would lie flat on the pillow and not ride up the pins, 'the pins should just find the hole and then be pressed back slanting away from the worker before being pressed firmly into the hole'. The pins on the headside and footside should slant outwards and as pins were taken from the back of the work to use again these should stay in longer than the others. I learnt how important the control of tension was; that pulling the footside too tight made a curved edge; that thread must hang evenly and not too long on the bobbins if the lace is to have an even texture. Lacemakers who saw a pillow with its bobbins hanging low, 'long as waggin whips', saw there a poor lacemaker.

Miss Channer always emphasised the importance of good quality linen thread for making point ground lace and saw the introduction of cotton thread as one of the causes of the decline in the quality. The development of a fine cotton thread for lace had been commended by the Buckinghamshire and Northamptonshire manufacturers as early as 1815. Cheaper than linen thread and easier to work, it came into general use from the 1830s, as the lacemakers tried to compete with the new machine-made laces. At both Northampton and Bedford she had stocked the finest linen threads she could get and all the work I did with her was in fine linen thread.

From time to time she revealed terms she had heard used by the older lacemakers, 'learning a lace' which meant working out the first head of a new pattern on the pillow; 'stitch around the pin' an earlier term for 'covering the pin'. Most of these have now been recorded in articles and books and will be known to present-day lacemakers who continue to add their own variants.

These Saturday afternoons gave me a great deal more than an elementary skill in lacemaking. As she demonstrated a stitch or watched me place a pin Miss Channer might recall some incident she had been told by one of the older lacemakers in her youth, or something she had learned of the other specialised crafts which supplied the lacemakers' needs, the bobbin makers, the pillow makers who had already almost disappeared by the time she and Miss Roberts were working.

As she shared these experiences and recollections with me the whole industry as well as the craft of lacemaking came to life. Other enthusiasts, contemporary with Miss Channer, had worked to revive and maintain lacemaking in the area, but few I think had her understanding of it as an industry. Looking back on our meetings now I regret that I did not ask her more about her own work between 1900 and 1940 and about the Lace Associations, but I was more interested then in earlier years and her recollections of that older generation of lacemakers. They had told her of their early days and what she was now telling me was of lacemakers of the 1830s and 1840s, putting me in touch with them at one remove. I hoped too that she would write her own account of these years—a sequel to *Lace-making in the Midlands*. But she was always reticent, modest about her own achievements, and thought that few people would in the early 1940s be interested in what had become an obsolete industry and an unfashionable craft. Yet only a few years after her death in 1949 a new edition of her other book, *Practical Lacemaking*, was issued and a lacemaking revival had begun. However, *Lace-making in the Midlands*, long out of print has not, until now, been reprinted.

Lace-making in the Midlands Past and Present

AN INTRODUCTION

The book begins with a brief historical account of lacemaking in Europe and in England. The lace of the East Midlands is then dealt with in a little more detail. Many books covering this ground in various ways have now been published, but what is written here can still hold its own as a clear, simple introduction to the subject. The first chapter, on European lace, gives an account of the technical development of the craft through its different origins and the influence of different ways of working on each other before it became classified geographically; 'for the earlier lace.... the system of place names is most confusing and tiresome' (p. 43).

In the second chapter, on the early history of lace in England, the authors do not appear to dissent from the tradition which first appeared in print in Mrs Palliser's *History of Lace* (1865) that Queen Katherine of Aragon, who died in 1536, encouraged the making of lace in Bedfordshire. They offer in support of it the existence of a lace in 'what we should call an old Italian pattern' made at Paulerspury and called 'Queen Catherine lace' (p. 45 and *Fig.* 7). Yet they have already placed the beginning of pillow-lace making in Europe in the latter half of the sixteenth century (p. 32). Later studies still do not suggest that patterns of this kind appeared before the late sixteenth century.

Mrs Palliser wrote of 'certain traditions handed down in the county villages of a good queen who protected their craft, the annual festival of the workers.... combined with the residence of that unhappy queen for the space of two years at her jointure manor of Ampthill lead us to infer that the art of lacemaking, as it then existed, was first imparted to the peasantry of Bedfordshire, as a means of subsistence, through the charity of Queen Catherine of Aragon.' No genuine folk tradition can be entirely disregarded, but· according to Mrs Palliser the actual tradition is 'of a good

21

queen'. It could be a much later queen, for instance Queen Adelaide, wife of William IV, who did make a point of wearing English lace.

Later research has failed to find any early reference connecting the East Midlands industry with Katherine of Aragon but since Mrs Palliser's book was published and re-issued several times since 1865 what she suggested has been repeated as historical fact. The Queen was at Ampthill in 1533, that is well recorded, and had no doubt been there from time to time earlier in Henry's reign. So the tradition of her presence in Ampthill is a real one. For her charity to the poor and her skill in embroidery there is contemporary evidence. The Bedfordshire lacemakers did celebrate St Katherine's day in the nineteenth century—if they weren't celebrating St Andrew's or St Thomas's day instead—because Katherine of Alexandria with her emblem of the wheel was the pre-Reformation patron saint of spinners and other textile workers. All this still does not amount to proof that Queen Katherine introduced lacemaking to the district.

Lace, as we now understand it, had hardly emerged as a distinct fabric from the needlework seamings and open-work embroidery into needlepoint lace, and from woven braids into bone (bobbin) lace. The 'laces' of the early sixteenth century were the functional laces used for fastenings, flat like tape or round like cord. Mrs Palliser does qualify the lace she is writing about here by saying 'as it then existed'. Lace as a decorative fabric only begins to appear in the mid sixteenth century, when it can be seen in portraits, and the earliest references to bone lace in England so far discovered are from this time. There are references to its wearing from the 1540s; to bone lacemakers in London from the 1560s; but not until the end of the century to its making in the East Midlands. Thomas Fuller writing in 1662 confirms this dating, 'Modern is the use thereof in England not exceeding the middle of the reign of Queen Elizabeth' (*Worthies of England*, p. 240).

Chapters 3 and 4 are on the lace schools and lacemakers. The older lacemakers in Spratton and Ravensthorpe will have been children of the lace schools and chapter 3, based on their memories, is probably a collection of experiences rather than a description of one particular school. Miss Roberts wrote an account of the Spratton lace school in *Northamptonshire Notes and Queries, 1891*, and this was used by A. S. Cole in his *Report on Northampton, Buckingham and Bedfordshire Lacemaking* made in the same year. An account of this Spratton lace school appears again in the 1902 (4th) edition of Mrs Palliser's *History of Lace*.

The holidays referred to for this district are St Thomas's and St Andrew's day, although in chapter 5, on the lacemaker in her home, there is an account of the keeping of St Katherine's day in Podington and the neighbouring villages from Mrs Orlebar of Hinwick House. Referring again to the Katherine of Aragon tradition the authors point out that if the queen did introduce the craft 'it was certainly very different from the present pillow-work being probably an adaptation of needlepoint' (p. 60).

Chapters 6, 7 and 8, on 'things exactly as they were' are as much a contribution to social history as to the history of lacemaking. The authors write from first-hand experience. They saw what the decline of the industry meant in the villages around Northampton, the added hardship it brought to their poorer neighbours. Writing on this decline in chapter six they do not place all the blame within the industry and on the competition of machine-made lace. 'The social change in village life had probably a far greater effect on the industry than had imitation laces' (p. 65). They are referring to the effects of the agricultural depression that struck the English countryside in the 1870s and 1880s. This was a result of competition to English farming from overseas, which brought cheaper wheat from America and cheaper frozen meat from Argentina and New Zealand.

Whether or not the agricultural depression contributed to the decline of the lace industry, together they brought hardship to both agricultural labourer and lacemaker. Earnings from lacemaking had for a long time been needed by many families to provide them with a bare subsistence. A desperate need to turn lace into money for food at the earliest opportunity—even if food were now a little cheaper—did not encourage the making of fine, time-consuming

lace. Miss Channer and Miss Roberts do not spare those who took advantage of this double hardship to depress the price of lace still further, 'People talk of having sometimes bought a bit of lace from some poor starving old woman, as if they had performed a great act of charity, instead of having got a fine piece of work for less than half its value' (p. 65). It was such exploitation and devaluation of the lacemakers' skill which moved them and others to the action recorded here in the last two chapters on the revival of the industry and its conditions and prospects in the late 1890s.

The Lace Associations and their ways of working reflect the social conditions of village life in the lacemaking counties in the 1880s and 1890s. The setting up of the Midland Association, the early years of its working and its problems are given here in a piece of first-hand reporting with a lively sense of involvement that no later writer could recapture. Miss Channer and Miss Roberts shared the enthusiasm and aims of the Association but were aware of the 'want of method.... and waste of force' which arose from the clash of wills and temperaments, combined with inexperience, as individual efforts were drawn together in support of a failing industry. The reader can still sense their simmering frustrations as they record the indifference and negative attitudes which met requests for support from official sources. They knew that technical instruction in lacemaking must be available if lacemaking was to continue as a small industry, producing good quality lace for a limited market; and that this could not be left to voluntary efforts. They saw the new Buckinghamshire Association learning from the mistakes of the Midland Association, but the book ends on a note of uncertainty for the future of lacemaking.

————————

PLATE 3. (On preceding page) Point ground lace designed by Miss Channer; worked by Mrs Dixon of Clapham, Bedford, at one of the classes of the Bedford Technical Institute, c. 1926. Actual size 340 mm x 250 mm. (*Cecil Higgins Art Gallery, Bedford*)

LACE-MAKING
IN THE MIDLANDS
PAST AND PRESENT

AT WORK
OLD FASHIONED PILLOW AND STAND
This girl was not a lacemaker at all but was dressed and posed for the photograph
'with a good deal of giggling, etc.'—information from Miss K. Richards.

LACE-MAKING

IN THE MIDLANDS

PAST AND PRESENT

BY

C. C. CHANNER

AND

M. E. ROBERTS

METHUEN & CO.

36 ESSEX STREET, W.C.

LONDON

1900

PLATE 4. Facsimile of the title page of the original edition of *Lace-making in the Midlands*. (*Luton Museum*)

FIG. 1
CUT WORK OR GREEK LACE, 16TH CENTURY

I

SKETCH OF THE PROGRESS OF
LACE-MAKING IN EUROPE

THE HISTORY of lace-making is the history of an art. A piece of lace is
an artistic composition expressed in twisted thread, just as a piece of
wood-carving is the expression of the artist's idea in chiselled wood.
Lace is not, like embroidery, an ornamented fabric; it is itself
ornament. It is not application of art to a craft; the whole pattern is the
fabric, and the fabric is the pattern. It is this peculiarity that
distinguishes lace from needlework and from woven-work.

The art is a comparatively modern one. No trace of it can be found
on ancient monuments or in early records; the term "old lace" is a
relative term, for before the sixteenth century nothing that we should
call "lace" existed.

It was about the close of the seventeenth century that lace reached
perhaps its highest point as a vehicle for the expression of artistic ideas.
About the middle of the sixteenth century pattern-books began to be
published, and it was the effort to carry out the ideas of the designers
of patterns which perfected the craft of lace-making. In form, in line,
in composition, the patterns belonging to the best periods of lace-
making are among the most perfect works that artistic design can
show.

Without good design lace becomes worthless rubbish, like a picture
without drawing.

In seeking to discover the origin of the art we find two distinct but
equally important sources. The first is the ornamentation of linen by
means of drawn-thread work and cut-work; the second is the twisting
of threads into narrow ornamental braids, known as lace or "purling."

Drawn-thread work, at least in its simpler forms, is familiar to most
people. When very fine and elaborate it has much the same effect as a
closely-worked piece of lace. Cut-work, or Greek lace as it is
sometimes called, is less familiar [*Fig. 1*]. It is formed by cutting out in
linen patterns, usually geometrical, and then closely button-holing
over the threads which remain. Take away the linen foundation from

31

the drawn-thread work and from the cut-work and you have a true needlepoint lace.

The second source of which I spoke is purling. Purling was a method of plaiting threads into a little looped edging, and the little loops so often to be found at the edge of lace are still called "purls." Purling is mentioned in the *Canterbury Tales*, and it was much used in the fifteenth century as an ornamental edging.

Other edgings called lace were also made. We should now call them fancy braid, but we still use the old word when we speak of "gold lace."

"Purling" and "lace" are pillow lace in embryo; but pillows, bobbins, and pins were not yet invented. These old lace-makers placed their balls of thread in a man's hand, using his fingers as pegs to assist in the plaiting and twisting. By employing two men fifteen or twenty threads could be used at once. What a laborious method of obtaining so small a result, we think, as we lightly hang our hundred or more bobbins on to the modern pin!

The early pin was large, and was made of boxwood or bone, not well adapted for lace-making. Their manufacture rapidly improved, and though they remained expensive articles of luxury they were, to a certain extent, in common use about the latter part of the sixteenth century. It was about this period that pillow lace-making commenced.

With the use of pin and pillow the early edgings became elaborated into something more like modern lace edgings, and they were probably made in England, as well as in Italy, Flanders, and other countries. A modern torchon edging is not unlike the Italian edging of the sixteenth century, as the use for such simple ornament has not passed away [*Fig. 2*].

Before proceeding to describe the further progress of lace-making we must draw particular attention to this method of twisting threads into a pattern to form an edging, as we shall frequently need to refer to it again.

We notice that it is an outcome of the fancy braid, and that there is no distinction between pattern and ground. The pattern can easily be pricked out on lines at an angle of 45° drawn on the parchment.

The threads are kept in place by means of pins, and are continuous; that is to say, each thread can be traced zigzagging through the whole

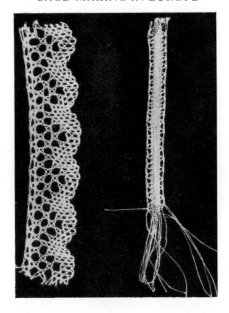

FIG. 2

TORCHON EDGING BRAID

length of the lace and lace-work, across the width of the edging from side to side, just as one would plait a dozen strands of straw. I shall in future term this method "working across the pattern," in order to distinguish it from the method of following the separate lines of the pattern which we shall find in some of the elaborate pillow laces.

In describing the edgings we have wandered far from the ornamental linen-work which we mentioned as one of the sources of the art of lace-making.

Though this book deals with pillow lace, and the linen-work of Italy was more immediately the parent of needlepoint lace, it is none the less important to us. Needlepoint and pillow lace were developed side by side, first in Italy and Flanders, and afterwards in France. The same lace-making districts often produced both needlepoint and pillow work; the same patterns often serve for either. Many pillow stitches are imitations of needle stitches; without the influence of needlepoint it seems likely that purling and lace-making would never have progressed beyond the making of narrow fancy edgings.

It will be interesting to trace the evolution of the various kinds of pillow lace, the interdependent development of pattern, stitch, and method. This evolution we will regard as *being entirely independent of* the art of making the simple edgings already explained.

In the oldest Italian or Flemish lace of any importance we find that the foundation of the fabric is a braid or tape. This braid, made with bobbins and pins on a pillow, takes the place of the button-holing which forms the solid part of needlepoint lace; it follows the curves and lines of the pattern, and the various turns and curves are connected by means of "sewings" [*Fig. 3*].

The sewing, as now practised by Honiton and Brussels lace-workers, is formed by catching a thread through a pinhole in an adjacent piece of braid and passing another thread through the loop thus formed. In this way a pattern worked in separate narrow lines is all joined into a homogeneous whole. Sometimes, instead of the braids being closely united, two threads are twisted, or four threads are plaited, into a little *bar* or "bride," fastened with a sewing into a part of the pattern at some distance and then carried back into the braid. These brides or connecting bars are a marked feature of some needlepoint lace, though of course here they are made in quite a different manner.

The manner in which the braid is carried round the curves is extremely ingenious, and very superior to the later methods of Honiton and Brussels workers. By working partly across the braid and then returning to the outer edge of the curve a kind of wedge can be formed, which brings the work round flat without any apparent thickening of the material. There are many old patterns, like the illustrations, in which the lines of the pattern are continuous, but this is not necessary [*Figs 3 and 5*]. By ending a braid and beginning another in a different part of the parchment, by cutting off bobbins or adding them, in order to alter the width of the lines, any pattern published by the designers could be followed. Many fancy stitches, some taken from the edging laces, were used to vary the monotony of the plain

FIG. 3

ITALIAN LACE WITH CONTINUOUS BRAID
CLOSELY CONNECTED WITH SEWINGS

braid, and purls like the purling of the fourteenth century could be worked along its edge.

While needlepoint lace was first confined to geometrical patterns, the braid lent itself to curves, and pillow lace may have for a time led the way in the improvement of patterns. In the seventeenth century patterns of both kinds of lace developed rapidly; from curves and scrolls we go on to stems, leaves, and flowers, and even animals and men appear—beautiful little drawings worked out in lace [*Fig. 4*].

Needlepoint lace, instead of consisting only of solid work and brides, begins to show "fillings-in" or "modes"—delicate open-work stitches which form the centres of flowers, etc.

Pillow lace was not left behind. It was a simple matter to curve a braid into the form of a flower; then, by means of sewings, threads could be attached to the edge of the braid and the flower centre filled with open-work stitches to rival the modes of the needlepoint.

Perhaps it will be as well to remark, in passing, that about this time needlepoint workers sometimes used a plain pillow braid, and, sewing it on to their patterns, joined and ornamented it with their stitches, thus saving themselves the labour of working the solid part of their pattern.

This kind of work was revived in this century, and was known among lady fancy-workers as "point lace." The work was often beautifully done, and the patterns good, but it is always inferior in effect to genuine needlepoint lace or to pillow lace of the same style. The pleats and gatherings in the braid are a great blemish.

In the middle of the seventeenth century lace with a net ground appears. Hitherto, though patterns had become elaborate, and fillings were common, and the variety of stitch in pillow lace was marvellous, the *net* ground was unknown. We must also remind ourselves that there was no "working across the pattern" in real "point", or lace as we should now call it. Every line of the pattern was followed separately, the various parts of the work being connected by sewings.

Flemish lace began to be extremely fine, and with the fine thread the necessity for the careful turning of the curves ceased, and the method was gradually forgotten. Though we see less of the absolutely continuous line, patterns remained of a continuous scrolling nature; it was the introduction of net which helped to cut patterns up till lace

FIG. 4

ITALIAN PILLOW LACE, 17TH CENTURY

FIG. 5
CONTINUOUS BRAID PATTERN
WITH FILLINGS AND PLAITED NET

ceased to be a pattern and became an arrangement of separate sprigs on a net ground.

The use of braid had at first suggested continuous lines, but it was soon found possible to work a single leaf by the same method, attach it to a stem, cut off the bobbins, and begin again elsewhere with another leaf or flower.

With the introduction of lace-making into other European countries came further developments. It seems that when the art is introduced into a new home it never remains the same, but always becomes in some way characteristic of its new sphere; so that we find Italian lace, Belgian lace, French lace, English lace, all perfectly distinct from one another. Fine Flemish lace introduced into Devonshire becomes the characteristic Honiton lace, and the lace of Lille and Valenciennes, imitated in the Midlands, becomes the Buckinghamshire point.

A symmetrical arrangement of brides and the open-work fillings no doubt led to the invention of net, which appears both in needlepoint and pillow lace.

The illustration [*Fig. 5*] shows the earliest form of pillow net. The pattern is worked first, then threads are attached to the edge of the braid and the ground is covered with net. This stitch is an extremely intricate one when compared to the modern Buckinghamshire "point ground", but it is not to be wondered at when it is understood that this net can be worked without the help of a single pin or so much as a line drawn on the parchment. The Midland lace-maker of to-day, unaccustomed to any but her own methods, is astonished and sceptical on hearing of net without pins; but in the early seventeenth century pins were not cheap, and the idea of keeping a twisted net in place by means of a forest of pins was undreamed of. Instead of twists, every side of this mesh is composed of four plaited threads; one couple is carried through from mesh to mesh to keep all firm and in place. Much must depend in such work on skill of hand and eye, and it is a slow, laborious stitch, but there is a fascination in the shaping of those hexagons which is wanting to the mechanical twisting of thread and sticking of endless pins.

As the seventeenth century proceeds, net grounds become commoner, and endless varieties appear, but the mesh is always plaited, not twisted.

By the time we reach the beginning of the eighteenth century we can associate a particular mesh with a particular lace-making district; the net is simpler, and begins to require immense numbers of pins.

Lace is now finer, and is worked in narrower widths than was the old Italian and Flemish lace. The patterns become much more detached. The lace of Mechlin and of Brussels, the ground of which is very similar, continues to be worked in pieces, the pattern first and the ground afterwards, but a very remarkable change is seen in the Valenciennes lace and in various French laces. This change is shown in a piece of lace in the South Kensington Museum marked as Dutch [*Fig. 6*]. It closely resembles Flemish lace with a net ground, but the ground is worked at the same time as the pattern; that is to say, threads are brought out of the pattern to form the net and carried back again into the pattern, so that the threads do not follow the lines of the pattern, but come in and out of it as convenient. In fact, the lace is worked like an edging on a large scale. Such a method requires an enormous number of pins, because every thread must be kept in place till the whole width of the pattern is worked. In the older method the twisted edge of the finished pattern was like the selvedge of a piece of woven material, and pins could quickly be moved forward to the point where the work was proceeding. By the old method it was almost as easy to work a piece of lace half a yard wide as a piece three inches wide. It was only a matter of time; the line was followed curve by curve and would never be of great width or need a very large number of bobbins.

It is easy to see how Flemish patterns led to the new plan. They are characterised by a peculiar flatness and closeness; lines are often marked in the plain work by means of little rows of twists in the working threads. It was seen that if an outline could be marked by twisted threads the same principle might be applied to the whole pattern; it might all be worked in one, the twisting of the threads outlining the design. There are some pieces of lace in the South Kensington Museum, labelled "Fausse Valenciennes", which show the progress of this method. They have the flat look of Valenciennes lace; there is very little distinction between pattern and ground—in fact, there is no true ground, the small space between the different parts of the pattern being covered with a filling-in. Valenciennes lace has to this day retained a simulation of the twisted selvedge edge of the braid, each

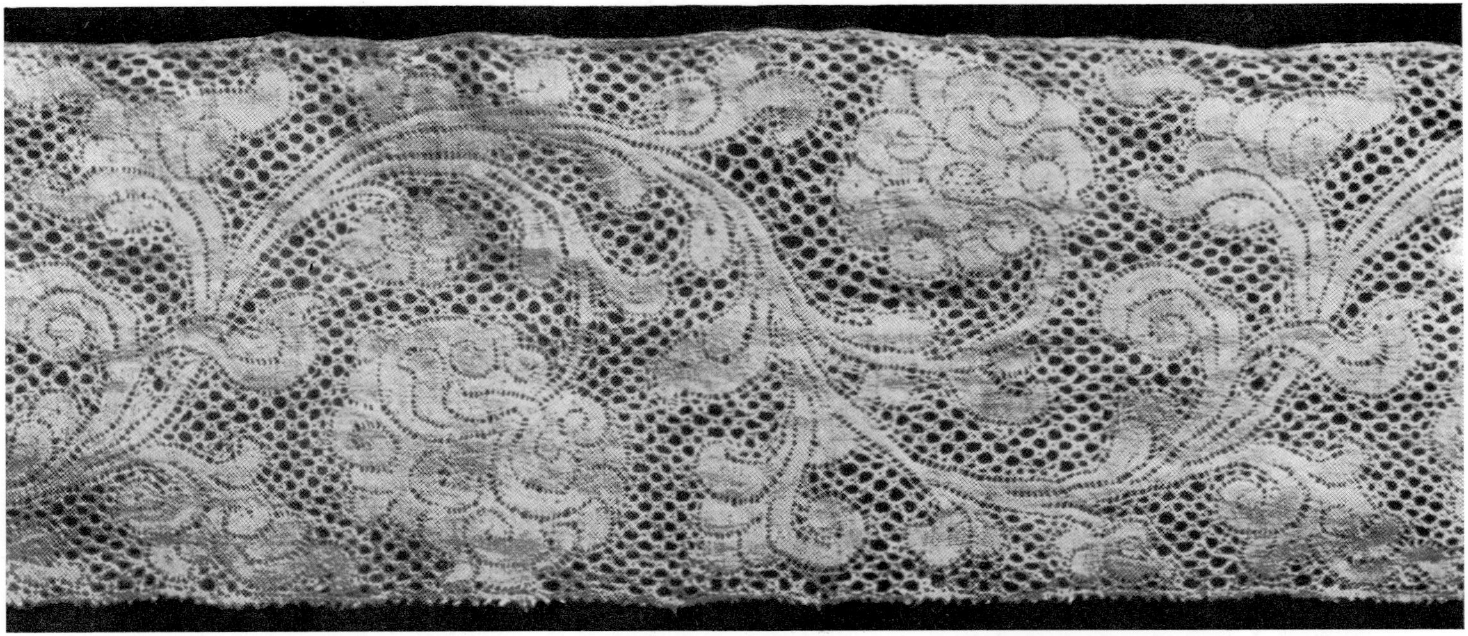

FIG. 6
DUTCH LACE

part of the pattern being surrounded by *simulated* pin-holes. In the lace of Lille we find the attempt to *imitate* the braid edge frankly abandoned; the pattern is kept distinct from the ground by running a thick white thread called a "gimp" round it. This gimp, which appears in Buckinghamshire lace, must not be confounded with the raised "cordonnet" which sometimes outlines the pattern in Brussels lace. The cordonnet, or "raised work", of Honiton lace is merely used to give boldness and relief, whereas the gimp is an essential part of a point-ground pattern "worked all across" the parchment.

During the eighteenth century fine pillow laces with net grounds reached their highest point of excellence, and began to be imitated by various kinds of embroidery on machine-made net known as "tambour work" and "Limerick lace".

During the nineteenth century the finest and best laces have made but little progress, but there has been a remarkable development of the torchon edgings. In almost every European country a great deal of heavy linen lace is made for the ornamentation of household linen. These laces are usually of geometrical design and are improvements on the old lace edgings, much having been learnt both in the way of workmanship and design from the true pillow points.

In the nineteenth century, then, we find a curious assimilation of the lace edging with the "point" or "passement", and we apply the same word "lace" to all ornamental fabrics of twisted and plaited thread. Let us briefly recapitulate the various steps by which this has been brought about.

Under the influence of needlepoint the ornamental braid was curved and shaped into a pattern, the various lines of the pattern being connected by sewings. The pattern became more shaped and elaborated, the brides became more ornamental and a more important part of the lace, ornamental fillings were introduced, and the work became, not a curved braid, but an arrangement of flowers and leaves—at first conventional, afterwards naturalistic. Then the net ground becomes general, and early in the eighteenth century some laces began to be worked all in one—pattern and ground as one fabric, without joins. It was now worked like a wide edging, a great many pins and a great many bobbins being employed. The only difference remaining was that the edging usually retained the geometrical pattern with the homogeneousness of pattern and ground; it still showed its character as an ornamental braid of interlaced threads. Even when a real point ground is so narrow as to be *used* as an edging its character is still obvious, and it cannot be confounded with a torchon edge.

In this short history of lace-making the aim has been not to give a history of the various lace centres, with a classification of lace by its place-name, but to show how the fabric itself grew into being and changed in nature, whether in Italy, France, or England. It is desired to show how a classification might be made, according to pattern and method of working, which would be of great use and interest to the lace-maker. Unfortunately there is a great lack of suitable technical terms for such a purpose.

The old place-names, such as Valenciennes, Brussels, or Lille, are of great value and interest, because they *do* indicate a special method and style; but for the earliest lace, which was much the same in Italy or Flanders, and probably in some other countries, and for modern lace, the system of place-names is most confusing and tiresome. Improved torchon lace is now made in Italy, Germany, Austria, Belgium, Switzerland, and England—in fact, almost all over Europe; patterns are carried from place to place, and there is little difference in the workmanship. Any lace may be made in any district—in point of fact, lace very like Brussels is made in Italy.

Something has been done of recent years to revive the manufacture of the finer and more important pillow laces. There is now a certain demand for copies of beautiful old lace, but it has not become a living, thriving industry. There can be no great sale for lace as a work of art as long as it is only an imitation.

The lace makers and designers of old were real artists, and their patrons were willing to spend great sums of money on lace. The small sums of money paid for the very best lace now make it useless for the artist to give his attention to the design, or for the lace-maker to put her best and most careful work into the execution of that wonderful web of plaited thread which some of us still love, and which unfailingly brings to its workers many happy and peaceful hours of never-wearying occupation.

II

THE PROGRESS OF LACE-MAKING IN ENGLAND
WITH SPECIAL REFERENCE
TO THE MIDLAND COUNTIES

IN THE preceding chapter we have roughly traced the evolution of lace-making in Europe; we must now seek to discover, in equally rough outline, the place which England holds among the lace-making nations. This place is by no means so unimportant as is sometimes represented, though the English love of French fashions has to a certain extent militated against the popularity of the purely English. Whatever difficulties in the way of good organisation of the industry we may have had to contend with, want of artistic feeling and originality cannot fairly be laid to the charge of the English lace-makers. Though often adopting French ideas from the foreign lace imported, in order to follow the foreign fashions, they have never been mere copiers. English designers, or drawers as they were called, have produced some most graceful and beautiful designs, and English workers have shown great dexterity in the adaptation of stitch and method to design. The result of an attempt to copy a foreign lace has usually been the production of a new and individual style by a natural process of development and artistic invention. This rule has been noticeable in Maltese lace, which in workmanship, texture, and design became, in English hands, a very different product from the original simple and rather coarse lace of Malta.

If artistic feeling, as is sometimes said, is shown in the workman's ornamentation of his tools, England stands pre-eminent. An intense pride in the ornamentation and arrangement of her pillow has always been a remarkable characteristic of the Midland lace-maker. More than 400 different patterns of decorated bobbins have been collected, and doubtless many more could be found.

In considering England's place as a lace-making nation we must remember that in other countries a great deal of the best lace was made in convents, and that in England it was impossible to fill the place of the cultured ladies to be found within convent walls. The convent was like a joint-stock company; it had capital both in money and in ability; it was

also a most convenient centre for the teaching of art and craftsman-
ship; and it had a commanding position as a commercial house. It was
manufacturer, merchant, capitalist, and instructor all at the same time.
The decline of convents in England left the lace industry with but little
capital and organisation; and both teaching and design generally
remained in the hands of a few families who understood it and in
which it was handed down from generation to generation.

Needlepoint, which requires more delicate skill of hand and eye than
does pillow lace, died out entirely as an article of English manufacture,
though we know that it was made in England in the sixteenth century;
the making of it was doubtless taught in the convents. There is a
tradition in the Midlands that Queen Catherine of Aragon worked
hard to encourage it in the villages, and that she introduced new
patterns. It is possible that she tried to teach pillow lace also, for there is
a pattern made in Northamptonshire, very like what we should call an
old Italian pattern (merely meaning that it is an early form of pillow
lace), which is called Queen Catherine's pattern [*Fig.* 7]. There is no
other Midland lace like it. It is said that she bade her ladies burn their
lace that they might buy of the poor English workers. Probably want
of encouragement and good technical instruction caused the industry
to die out after her death. England was soon plunged into the Puritan
abyss which almost killed art. We spoke in our previous chapter of the
purling mentioned by Chaucer, and of the lace edgings which
suggested the use of pillow and bobbins for the true "point". These
edgings were extensively made in England, and were known as "bone
lace". The word "lace" would not have been applied to the wide points
which were the rivals of needlepoint.

In *Twelfth Night* Shakespeare shows his familiarity with the sight of
lace-makers—

> "*Duke.* O fellow, come, the song we had last night;
> Mark it, Cesario, it is old and plain:
> The spinsters and the knitters in the sun,
> And the free maids that weave their thread with bones,
> Do use to chaunt it."

About 1662 Flemish workers were brought to England to teach their
superior kind of lace. The industry took root in Devonshire and
became the famous Honiton lace. This must have seemed to the bone-

lace makers a very new and different kind of work from the weaving of their edgings. Honiton lace soon developed a style of its own, but though much beautiful Honiton work has been done the design is often poor. It is curious that Midland lace has never suffered from this poverty of design; it was not so far from the great trade routes, it is more adaptable to any form of pattern, and it requires greater technical skill to make a point-ground (Buckinghamshire) parchment. Any good design, either conventional or naturalistic, can be worked in point-ground lace, but some styles are impossible in Honiton lace. On the other hand, within certain limits, Honiton lace is a better means of expression, and it is much easier to make the parchments. This last fact tempts persons with little powers of draughtmanship to make their own parchments, whereas the point-ground design must be left in the hands of the professional.

We have seen that needlepoint spread more quickly in Europe than pillow point. Honiton lace must have been one of the earliest of the transplanted pillow points. Next in point of time must have come French pillow laces, and then Buckinghamshire point. This lace shows French influence; it is worked all in one across the pattern, like a French lace; the selvedge edge to the pattern has been replaced by a gimp; the net is not of an early character, being a twisted net dependent on pins; none of it can be earlier than the eighteenth century. Some of the parchments are very like Valenciennes parchments, though we find no trace of the Valenciennes ground or the simulated "pin-holes". The introduction of this kind of lace greatly influenced the bone-lace makers, and gave rise, especially in Northamptonshire, to the manufacture of many charming little point-ground edgings, which, while sometimes remaining geometrical in design, resembled in workmanship the wide-point grounds of Bucks.

Maltese lace, introduced in this century, is a development of an edging founded on patterns of interlacing circles instead of the more usual intersecting straight lines.

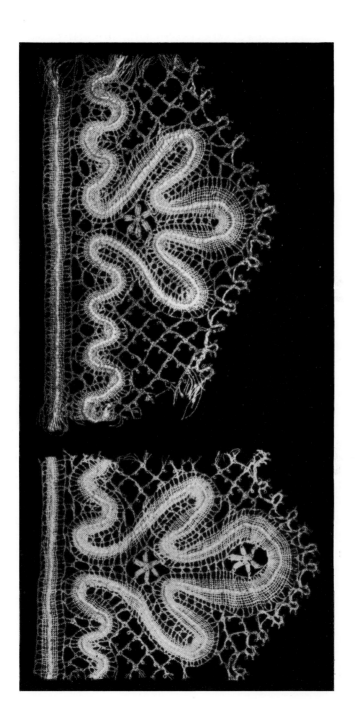

FIG. 7

CATHERINE OF ARAGON LACE

III

LACE-MAKING IN THE MIDLANDS
DURING THE EIGHTEENTH AND
NINETEENTH CENTURIES

"The pattern grows, the well-depicted flower,
Wrought patiently into the snowy lawn,
Unfolds its bosom: buds and leaves and sprigs,
And curling tendrils gracefully dispos'd,
Follow the nimble fingers of the fair—
A wreath that cannot fade of flowers that blow
With most success when all besides decay."
COWPER.

THE POET Cowper, living at Olney, the centre of one of the best lace-making districts, was familiar with the fine point-grounds of graceful flowery design, and his poetic muse was not neglectful of the lace-makers. The greater part of Buckinghamshire, Northamptonshire, part of Bedfordshire, and a little bit of Oxfordshire, form the lace-making district of the Midlands. These counties have always supported textile industries of one form or another, with a leaning towards dainty manufactures such as ribbons, straw-plaiting, or lace-making. Many Northamptonshire villages now given over to the unsightly shoe trade once lived by the weaving of plush and silk; other villages within living memory were occupied with darning net for window curtains, etc., the work being known as "frame-work".

The very small and dainty hands of many women in the North-amptonshire villages are often remarked upon by strangers; they are certainly an artistic race, showing it especially in their extreme fondness for flowers and appreciation of pretty scenery. From the beginning of the eighteenth century until the middle of the nineteenth, point-ground lace, generally known as Buckinghamshire point, became characteristic of the district. The best lace was made in the southern part of Northamptonshire near Towcester, and in Buck-inghamshire in and round Olney. Northampton and the western part of the county were famous for the narrow edgings and cheaper laces. Bedfordshire always appears to take to work of a showy daintiness. It became the home of Maltese lace, and now makes millinery laces of horsehair and tinsel, and twists beaded wire into patterns, and works with paillettes and spangles.

The improvement in lace-making which took place in the eighteenth century was partly due to the refugees who flocked to our shores after the revocation of the Edict of Nantes. This explains the very close resemblance between French and English pillow laces.

Defoe, writing of Bedfordshire, says: "Through the whole south part of this county, the people are taken up with the manufacture of bone lace, in which they have wonderfully exercised and improved within the last few years." He also mentions Newport Pagnell and other towns in Bucks as being the centres of much trade.

During the reigns of the Georges, notwithstanding much smuggling of foreign goods, the trade steadily increased, and at the marriage of Frederick, Prince of Wales, nearly all the lace worn was of English make.[*]

In 1750 the Society of anti-Gallicans was formed; it held quarterly meetings, and did much to encourage good work. Two years after it began, it awarded the first prize to Mr. William Marriote of Newport Pagnell for bone lace, which, according to the judges, was the best ever made in England. In 1761 the lace-makers of Bucks presented the King with a fine pair of lace ruffles. In 1763 good King George, always anxious for the welfare of his people, ordered that all stuffs and laces to be worn at his sister's wedding[**] should be made in this country; but the nobility preferred to disobey him, and ordered, as was their habit, a quantity of foreign material. What must have been their disgust and alarm on hearing that three days before the wedding the King had sent his custom-officers to the Court milliner to carry off the prohibited goods. But a lesson had been learnt, for on His Majesty's birthday the Court appeared in garments of strictly British make.

----

* However, the royal accounts 1739-50 show a preference for Mechlin and Brussels lace (Levey, p. 72 and 28).
** Princess Augusta, to Duke of Brunswick, 1764 (Palliser).

The fluctuations in the lace industry have always been remarkable, the scale of prices rising and falling in a bewildering and astonishing manner: at one time we hear of lace-makers earning £1 a week, at another time but 3s. or 4s.

In 1780 the trade seems to have fallen into a bad condition; for Cowper, enclosing a petition to Lord Dartmouth in favour of lace-makers, declares that "Hundreds in this little town (Olney) are upon the point of starving, and the most unremitting industry is barely sufficient to keep them from it."

For many years Cowper's house was used as a lace school under the management of Mrs. Langley, the wife of a former vicar; about forty workers were employed.

In 1785 an essay was published in the *Gentleman's Magazine* dealing with the cause of deformity among the lace-makers of Bucks and Northants, and suggesting certain remedies which have long since been adopted.

As at the beginning of the eighteenth century our laces owed much to France, so in the nineteenth we received another impetus from refugees who fled from the Revolution. When war was declared and our ports were closed against French goods, energetic buyers under-took to supply the English market with lace like that made in Normandy. The "French ground" was introduced, which resembles what is now known as "Point de Paris".

At Hanslope, in Bucks, 800 out of 1,275 inhabitants made lace, and a net profit of over £800 was yearly brought into the place. Those were grand times for the lace-makers, both men and women, many of them earning as much as £1 1s. per week; but this state of things did not last long, for the prices dropped when peace was made.

Queen Victoria is the possessor of some lovely English lace; a small piece, made for the Princess Royal when an infant, remains in the possession of a lace-buyer at Olney, where it was worked; a photograph of it is shown [*Fig. 8*].

The exhibition of 1851 brought about a revival of the lace industry. The wife of the lace-buyer above mentioned worked with one or two others at the exhibition. The pillows were covered for the occasion with blue velvet edged with rose colour and with rose-coloured bobbin bags. The lace worked by Mrs. Smith from the pattern shown in the

illustration [*Fig. 9*] took the gold medal prize. The lace was exquisitely fine, twenty slip thread being used, a degree of fineness almost unknown at the present day. It took three months to make one foot of lace. Her Majesty the Queen, after watching Mrs. Smith work, asked, as so many ladies ask lace-makers, why her bobbins were of so many different patterns: "Is it in order to tell which of them should be turned over?" These bobbins used in the presence of the Queen have been carefully treasured, though Mr. Smith has given many away to those

FIG. 9
DESIGN FOR BUCKS PILLOW LACE
WORKED BEFORE THE QUEEN AT
THE EXHIBITION OF 1851

who will value them. Some are in the posession of the authors. The few words uttered by Her Majesty have been remembered and repeated with ever-increasing interest through the years that have passed, and the kindly notice given by the sovereign marked the day as a red-letter day to the Olney lace-makers.

A woman now living in Spratton remembers the time when her mother, then living at Creaton, made the lace worn by the Lady Sarah Spencer at the wedding of the Princess of Wales [in 1863]. She was but a child, but remembers distinctly the lady coming on horseback now and again to see how the lace was getting on. She does not remember the price of it, but says that the money earned by her mother for this special piece of lace bought them a pony and trap, the first they had ever had.

About the close of the fifties Maltese lace was introduced into the Midlands, and in many places its manufacture unfortunately superseded the old points. It is more quickly made and will better bear the introduction of bad work than will the point ground. Perhaps, though much of it can have little claim to beauty, it is not altogether bad that it should have been introduced. It widened the ideas of the lace-makers, suggesting new methods and accustoming them to turn their hands to any kind of lace.

The last great outburst of prosperity was in 1870, owing to the Franco-German War, when lace-makers again earned splendid wages; but since then, until the present revival, with the exception of a short rage for "yak" lace, it had been at a very low ebb. In many villages the industry was almost entirely abandoned, and many workers had yards of beautiful lace of which they were quite unable to dispose.

IV

LACE SCHOOLS

I SHOULD be sorry to outrage the susceptibilities of my readers by suggesting that they could recall the early part of this century, but I am going to ask them if, in imagination *only*, they will be so kind as to go back through six or seven decades and visit with me one or two of the lace schools which were then scattered so thickly throughout the counties of Beds, Bucks, and Northants.

The first one that we enter strikes us as stifling, in spite of the door and the two windows being thrown open, and no wonder, for in that cottage-room are gathered thirty pupils, varying from six to sixteen years of age. The boys are dressed like the village lads of to-day, excepting that instead of knickerbockers they all wear trousers; but the girls have print frocks, low at the neck and sleeves, and very short in the skirt, from which peep white stockings and shoes, varying in neatness according to the disposition and means of the parents. Some of the children are very small, not more than six years of age.

They are sitting in rows, each little person on his or her four-legged stool, with its pillow resting against the three-legged stand in front of it. Those pillows are dressed in dark blue, and look as if they had tasted of the good things in life, so round are they, and fat, and heavy; indeed, when they carry them, the younger children's arms will hardly meet round them, and their little feet stagger under the weight.

In front of the thirty stools is a desk at which, in her majesty, is enthroned the teacher. But for the addition of spectacles and a kerchief she is dressed like the elder girls; by her side lies her sceptre, the all-powerful sceptre, her cane. Every hour she goes her rounds from pillow to pillow, and woe betide the luckless pupil whose work is badly done!

As the children turn the bobbins over and over, they sing doggerel verse called "tells", sticking pins as fast as their little fingers can plant them; at every tenth pin they call out the number, and so the room is full of counting. Now they have taken sides, and are going to "strive", or race each other, to see which can stick the greater number of pins in a given time. To escape the cane they have to put in ten pins a minute, or

600 an hour; but as the race grows in excitement many of them get in between 700 to 800, while we grow giddy at the sight, and at the sound of the ceaseless "clack, clack" of the bobbins.

It is nearly dinner-time. All but quite the little ones have been there since six o'clock; they are beginning to grow fidgety—visions of pie, cheese, and cake float over the parchments. At last comes the welcome news that "time's up". Each child covers over its pillow, turns its four-legged stool upside down, places the pillow in it, and runs off laughing and shouting, with the girls' straw or paste-board bonnets and bare necks gleaming in the sunshine.

All but a little girl of seven. She is scrupulously clean, but very small and delicate—a sweet little child, with long, fair hair hanging down her back in two tidy plaits. Her blue eyes, and very blue they are, just now are filled with tears; but the little white face is set in order to keep them from brimming over and spoiling her lace. She is faint and weak from one of those sick headaches to which poor children are so often subject. She has had nothing to eat since early morning, and, like all the others, excepting a few learners, has been working since six o'clock. As it neared the dinner-hour her spirits had revived, for had she not brought hers with her, and was it not now in the oven? Such a dinner too, gooseberry tart with sugar! Suddenly she had found herself on the floor, knocked down by the rough fist of her teacher. "I'll wake you! If you don't choose to work with the others, you'll have to stop in while they play."

At one o'clock the others troop in again and pack themselves in, row behind row, and work goes on as before, only the room grows hotter, and the "clack, clack" of the bobbins more monotonous. We wonder how the children can keep their attention. For the most part they sit very upright; for has not mother told them again and again that if they stoop over their work they will get hunchbacked?

Now and again a child falls short of pins, and goes "a-begging". Stopping before a likely giver, it sings "Mary Ann" (or whatever the name may be), "a pin for the poor; give me one, and I'll ask you no more". In this way it generally gathers for itself a nice little store.

Tea-time comes. Out run the children for half an hour; but the little figure by the window sits on, for her task is not done.

From five to six is a quiet time; you can hear a pin drop, for the children are working for dear life, many with aching backs and through a mist of tears. They know that if when "time's up" is called they should be but five pins behind they will be kept in another hour.

It is over, and the room is empty of all save three or four; but among them is the child by the window. She has had twelve hours of it; she is only seven, and suffering from want of food and a sick headache.

With a sigh we turn to watch the others, and hope that they now, after so many hours of hard work, are free to skip and play hop-scotch like their little grandchildren of to-day. But no; for many of them learning is not yet over: they are going to the night-school, where wearily they will pick up enough of reading to make in after life their leisure a blessing to them rather than a curse.

An hour later we pass a little blue-eyed child sobbing piteously. She has just been released from her work, and is holding in her arms her much-longed-for gooseberry tart; but alas! It is burnt to a cinder. She is an old woman now, but the memory of that disappointment is still fresh to her.

It is on a winter's evening that we visit our next school. As we enter we can make out some sixteen girls from the ages of seven to twenty, and we notice that they are all working by the light of one tallow candle. The little ones went home when it grew dark, and those who are left are mostly good workers.

In the centre of the room stands the four-legged candle-stool as high as an ordinary table. The top, which is called the "hole-board", is pierced by a hole in the centre and four others round it. In the middle hole is fixed a long stick with a socket for the candle at the top and peg-holes through the side, so that it can be raised and lowered at will. In the other four holes there are placed wooden cups, into each of which fits a flask made of very thin glass and filled with water. These flasks act as strong condensers or lenses. The girls sit diagonally, four to each bottle, those in the second and third circle having the better light.

The room, though stuffy, is cold, for, being so full, the fire has to be kept low. We wonder why the girls do not shiver more, for they are clad like their predecessors in print dresses, and from their low sleeves and large white collars gleam their bare necks and arms.

As usual they are singing. This time it is a "tell" that would be useful for all lace-workers to learn: "Do your stitch, stick your pin, and do your stitch about it." Indeed, it is for want of this "stitch about the pin" that so many workers' lace is faulty. Then they strike up another.

While they are singing, we will ask the teacher to tell us a little about the school, and to show us some of the lace they have made, and which is waiting to be taken to the lace-buyer, who lives in the neighbouring town.

When a little child joins the school she is usually six or seven, but sometimes one is taken who is a year or so younger. If she is sharp, she will be about three weeks learning her first little edging; during that time she pays 1s. a week, and afterwards 3d, in the summer, and 4d. during the winter (this varies a little in different schools, as do the hours of working). For the first six months she generally puts in only nine hours a day, but after that at least ten, with the exception of Saturday, which is a half-holiday. The winter hours are usually from eight to eight, allowing two hours for meals, but many work an hour or so longer. Every Saturday the teacher takes the lace to the buyer, and gives the girls the exact amount that they have earned, deducting only the 3d. or 4d. a week for the use of the room and lights. If they sell their work to a private customer, they are allowed to charge 1d. a yard more.

Then she shows us what they have made. First there is the little edging upon which the new-comers are started; it is called "the town trot". After that we see an array of the sweetest baby-laces, the narrowest being only 3d. a yard. Many of them are made up on the daintiest of baby-caps; for in those days babies began their lives in a staid and respectable manner, even wearing their caps under their hoods when they went out. Round the border of a cap ran one or two rows of narrow lace, plain or closely quilted in tiny box-pleats, while in the centre there is a lace "round" or "horseshoe", often exquisite in design and workmanship. Here is one set off by narrow loops of white satin ribbon. Then there are a set of cambric handkerchiefs and full-grown nightcaps, edged with the "heart" and "oak-leaf" patterns. After we have admired and wondered, she fetches a large wooden box, out of which she brings some truly lovely designs in rich lace handkerchiefs, parasol-covers, veils, etc. She tells us that the girls at her school usually earn, after deducting what they pay her, 2s. 3d. a week.

But you must not think that the teacher gives us this information all at once, for she constantly leaves us to inspect the workers. Sometimes she remarks to a girl, "I'll wake you! you've been asleep!" and wake her she does by a smart hit of her cane across the bare shoulders.

Just then a knock comes at the door—a father has come for his lass. It is a pity that there are not more like him, for the girls turned out into the darkness will find rough lads waiting round the corners for some of them, and so, hardly through their own fault, many come to sorrow.

It is St. Thomas's Day. The children are assembled; row behind row they are sitting, with their fat pillows resting against the stands before them. But by the look of repressed excitement on every face, there is evidently something about to happen. Presently the teacher leaves the room on the pretence of getting a parchment. In a minute the girl nearest the door has sprung up and bolted it; the pillows are put on one side, and an indescribable hubbub ensues. When the teacher returns she shakes the door violently, demanding to be let in; but the answer comes from thirty voices, "It's St. Thomas's Day; give us a half-holiday, and we'll let you in." For five minutes or so she stands outside grumbling and knocking, and then, finding that the children have turned the stools against her, she (not unwillingly, perhaps) gives in. The holiday is promised, the door is opened, and she walks in as the children rush out. As we watch them laughing and shouting, we think that it is a pity that custom should have fixed their holiday for one of the dullest and certainly the shortest of the days in the year.

"Are there any other days that you are turned out of your own school?" we ask the teacher. "No; but they generally manage to work half-time on St. Andrew's Day." "And what do they do with the other half?" "Oh, have tea in the schoolroom", she answers grimly. "It is the young folk who are spoilt nowadays."

After that we leave her to her pillow, with the click-clack of her bobbins sounding mournfully through the now deserted room.

V

LACE-MAKERS AT HOME

"Yon cottager, who weaves at her own door,
Pillow and bobbins all her little store;
Content though mean, and cheerful if not gay,
Shuffling her thread about the livelong day—
Just earns a scanty pittance, and at night
Lies down secure, her heart and pocket light."
COWPER

HAVING visited the lace schools, I will ask my readers if they will bear with me while I tell them a little about the workers of this century in their own homes. A child was often introduced to her pillow at three years old by her mother, and then, when she had learnt how to handle her bobbins, she was sent off to the lace school, where she would stay until she either went into service or was married; or, if she wished to save the expense of the 3d. or 4d. a week, she would work in her own home. In those days, especially in one part of the Midlands, nearly every cottager, married or single, sat at her pillow; for it was usually only farmers' or tradesmen's daughters who thought of going to service.

Whatever may be said of the "good old days", the results were most disastrous, not only to their health, but also to their morals; indeed, a lady, who is interested in a certain Midland village, tells me that although it was sad to see an old industry dying out, yet she was only too thankful when bad work and bad prices made it necessary for the girls to desert their pillows and go out into service. In this chapter we will endeavour to show how the present revival of the trade has been obtained without the slightest risk either to health or morals, and also how it is of benefit to many hundreds of families.

At the time of the Queen's accession [in 1837], as has been said, the trade was very flourishing, and it was found that a man could earn more at lace-making than in the fields, where his wages would be from 7s. to 8s. a week, while at his pillow he could make 9s. or 10s. In those days, then, workers, men and women, would sit side by side in each other's houses, in order to save firing. In the winter they had to sit very near to the windows, which did not give as much light as they do now, and it was often bitterly cold. In some parts, to keep themselves warm, they used a "dicky pot"; this was made of rough brown ware, glazed, and filled with embers begged from the bread oven of a well-to-do neighbour.

In print we often find mention of deformity and disease among lace-workers. These were greatly due, first, to the overcrowding of the schools, and secondly, to the constrained position necessarily adopted by men, women, and even babies, in order to see their work. No wonder, then, that a certain little boy in Bucks, one day growing disgusted, made away with his pillow down a well!

The patterns were usually designed and pricked either by lace-buyers, superior workers, or those brought up specially to that part of the trade, many of the designs, especially some drawn at Olney, being very lovely (See *Figs. 10 and 11*).

Here I should like to insert an account of the keeping of St. Catherine's Day, which was long held as a holiday both by lace-makers and weavers in parts of the Midlands. Its origin is probably far older than the time of Catherine of Aragon, but very possibly, being her fête-day, it has since been held in special honour by lace-makers, as tradition points to that queen as the introducer of the craft. If so, it was one certainly very different from the present pillow-work, being probably an adaptation of needlepoint.

I am indebted for the following account to Mrs Orlebar, of Hinwick House:--

"*Cattern Tea.*—In Podington and neighbouring villages the lace-makers have, within the memory of middle-aged people, 'kept Cattern' on December 6th—St. Catherine's Day (Old Style). I believe it was Catherine of Aragon who used to drink the waters of a mineral spring in Wellingborough, and who (as is supposed) introduced lace-making into Beds. The poor people know nothing of the Queen, only state that it was an old custom to keep 'Cattern.'

"The way was for the women to club together for a tea, paying 6*d*. apiece, which they could well afford when their lace brought them in 5*s*. or 6*s*. a week.

FIG. 10
DESIGN FOR CENTRE
OF BADGE CAP

FIG. 11
DESIGN FOR FINE BUCKS LACE
MADE AT OLNEY
EARLY 19TH CENTURY

"The tea-drinking ceremony was called 'washing the candle-block,' but this was merely an expression. It really consisted in getting through a great deal of gossip, tea, and Cattern cakes—seed cakes of large size. Sugar balls went round as a matter of course. After tea they danced, just one old man whistling or fiddling for them, and '*they enjoyed theirselves like queens!*'

"The entertainment ended with the cutting of a large apple pie, which they divided for supper. Their usual bedtime was about eight o'clock.

"An old rhyme is still extant about Cattern. I cannot recover more than these lines:—

> "'Rise, maids, arise!
> Bake your Cattern pies!
> Bake enough, and bake no waste,
> So that the old bell-man may have a taste!'"

VI

THE DECLINE OF THE LACE INDUSTRY

DURING the childhood of the now middle-aged in our villages the lace industry was flourishing and well paid; ten years ago the trade was almost extinct; but one generation separates us from the time when almost every child in the village was "brought up to the pillow."

What was the cause of this sudden decline, of this astounding change in village life? Ask an old lace-maker, and the reply will be, "Machine-made lace"; inquire a little further into the subject, and the inadequacy of the answer will strike you forcibly. The question is really a most complex one; it cannot be answered without some consideration of the great social changes which were taking place all over England in the earlier part of our Queen's reign. In this short book one cannot pretend to answer it thoroughly and satisfactorily.

Let us first try to understand in what way machine-made lace did really affect the industry. It must be borne in mind that the disappearance of English pillow-made lace from the market did not coincide in time with the production of good machine work, and also that we never ceased to import pillow lace from abroad, and further that the present revival of the pillow lace industry comes at a time when imitation lace of good quality can be had at very low prices.

Until the present century lace was essentially an adjunct of the rich. It was costly, of fine and intricate workmanship, and was prized accordingly. The wealthy and the noble possessed it, the middle class had a little, the poor did not aspire to lace at all. With the introduction of machine lace the fabric became common; the imitation was eagerly bought by those to whom the real thing had been an unhoped-for luxury, and to them it seemed almost as good and as beautiful. Many could not even distinguish between the hand work and the machine work.

A rage for cheap lace set in, and with it came the introduction of Maltese, which was showy and cheap compared to the point grounds [*Fig. 12*]. Pillow lace tried to compete with machine lace on its own

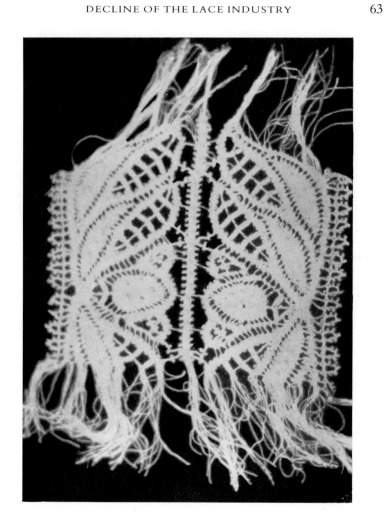

FIG. 12
MALTESE LACE
MADE IN MIDLAND COUNTIES

ground, that of cheapness and showy effectiveness. Until the public tired of Maltese and coarse edgings the lace-makers did not suffer—then the crash came. Machine lace improved, imitations of the beautiful old laces were produced; the public had not yet learnt to distinguish the true from the false, and the pillow lace-makers had all but forgotten how to make good lace. In the race for cheapness they had begun to use cheap cotton threads, and to work in a slipshod manner. Prices fell to a deplorable level, and lace-making came to be hated as the most fearful drudgery. Only a return to the good old lace and the good old methods could save the industry; it was found impossible to turn out bad lace as cheaply and as rapidly as the machine.

Some proof of the truth of these facts may be gathered by noting the extraordinary difference of opinion which exists among former lace-makers as to the merits of the trade. An old woman of seventy or eighty, whose memory goes back to the flourishing day of the beautiful point-ground lace, or half-stitch as it is sometimes called, will say, "Ah, I always loved my pillow. I shall always love it; I will work at it as long as I can sit to it and see." "Give me a pair of spectacles as I can see with," says another, "and let me have my pillow; it's nice work." "It's nice clean work," echoes another old body; "why don't the young folk take to their pillows now? we loved our pillows." In another cottage we hear, "When I was a girl I spent all my pocket-money on my pillow; I loved to have it nice. I had some beautiful bobbins, bone ones with beads on them and names, and my pins had different-coloured heads. How we loved our pillows, and what we would spend on them!" Now talk to a buxom widow of middle age: "I *hate* it; I burnt all my bobbins; it's a bad trade." "If you go lace-making," says another, "you'll never have salt to your porridge." "It's an awful trade, lace-making," we hear from another; "you'll never make your fortune at it. I always said none of my children should be lace-makers." The explanation of the contrast is to be found in the fact that the middle-aged remember the bad times, the cheap lace and poor patterns, the fearful hurrying and ceaseless work. The older women think of the time when the work was beautiful and good and a joy to do.

We cannot leave the subject of machine-made lace without remarking the injurious effect it has upon the public taste. When it aims at imitating the work of the pillow, the spurious showiness and perfection of it—the likeness and yet unlikeness—palls when one becomes accustomed to it, and may create a distaste for the real thing, which, in contrast to the imitation, never by itself tires the eye. This difficulty is met by the manufacturers by a constant change of fashion and style, the tawdriness of the new fashion passing unnoticed. Machine lace is at its best when it does not directly imitate any pillow lace, when it takes an independent place of its own, with suitable designs made expressly for it. The distinction between the real and the imitation is now much more clearly understood than it was twenty years ago; the true place and use of each is recognised, and, though real lace cannot regain the unique position which it once held, it cannot now be said to suffer from competition with the machine.

The social change in village life had probably a far greater effect on the industry than had the imitation lace. The small, self-supporting community had become little more than a colony of agricultural labourers. The Parish Councils failed to restore the village life because the old free population had departed into the towns, the little village trades were lost or merged in the great town manufactures. The change came gradually, and as it came it threw more and more power into the hands of the landowner and tenant farmer, and it was to their interest to discourage the village industry and made the population entirely dependent upon the land. We have many proofs of what was done to bring contempt upon the lace industry. Instead of any effort being made to prevent evil in connection with the lace schools the whole system was most unjustly condemned. Farmers' wives still speak contemptuously of lace-making, and twelve or fourteen years ago few of the landowners knew or cared anything about the trade. People talk of having sometimes bought a bit of lace from some poor starving old woman, as if they had performed a great act of charity, instead of having got a fine piece of work for less than half its value.

We asked a middle-aged woman for reminiscences of the lace school.

"I never went much to a lace school, though of course I made lace. Our clergyman's wife persuaded me to leave the lace school and come to a school she had, to learn needlework."

No doubt there was much of this persuading and much demonstration of the superiority of the needlework to lace, and the greater
respectability of the lady's school.

No one can do too much in the cause of true education, but it was
characteristic of the times that the way to improve the girls should have
been the destruction of a beautiful craft. The reform of the lace school
was perhaps as necessary as the reform of the factory. We know more
now of the merits of fresh air and space; but the teachers were not
always tyrants, and the best of our village population—the most
refined and clever and enterprising—spent their childhood at their
pillows.

The rôle of the former lace-makers numbers National School
teachers, shopkeepers, and the wives of the higher rank of village
artisans. It can hardly be argued that the trade was the enemy of
education.

The Education Act dealt the final blow at the lace industry. The
school at Paulers Pury, in Northants, was continued until after the
children were obliged to attend the National School; but it had to be
abandoned, as the teacher (who still makes lace) found that her pupils
were not able to do any good work after the day's lessons were over.
They were thus left without technical training, everything being given
up for the sake of learning reading, writing and arithmetic.

At Paulers Pury the best point-ground work had always been
made—work which no machine could rival, and which was always
valuable; and the direct effect of the Education Act and of the
changing social conditions is most clearly seen [*Fig. 13*].

The loss of the lace schools left the industry without organisation
and without capital and without a fresh supply of trained workers.
After a bad period of idling at home, the girls began to go out to service
and to take the place of the tradesmen's and farmers' daughters, who
were beginning to think domestic service beneath them. To go out was
now considered a rise in the social scale, and so the contempt in which
lace-making was held increased.

In the next chapter we shall endeavour to follow the turn of the tide
which has resulted in the revival of the old trade.

FIG. 13
PILLOW LACE, 19TH CENTURY
NOW MADE AT PAULERS PURY

VII

REVIVAL OF THE LACE INDUSTRY

IT HAS been felt for some time past that something must be done to prevent the utter stagnation of village life, and that to provide a good school with nothing beyond but the work on the land was to sow the seeds of discontent and the mischief that comes of dulness. We have been encouraging village entertainments and holidays, village music, and, above all, village industries. The Home Arts and Industries Association for Northamptonshire, under Miss Dryden's energetic influence, has done wonders for the lace as well as for other beautiful crafts. Other county exhibitions have encouraged lace-making competitions, and it is usually an important feature at the great annual Home Arts and Industries Exhibition at the Albert Hall.

Even before this great movement ladies were beginning to interest themselves in the beautiful but almost vanished craft of the Midland counties. Old lace-makers who remembered how to make the delicate baby-laces of a former generation were sought out and set to work. Marvellous parchments for the old wide half-stitch patterns, long thrown aside for the coarse Maltese, were discovered and wondered at. Harrowing tales were told of parchments burnt, or boiled down to make glue, and of bobbins used to light the fire. The inquiring ladies, under the spell that lace seldom fails to throw over its devotees, sought out good threads and patterns, and eagerly bought up good work.

A poor old widow, seventy-nine years of age, when visited by one of the ladies who was hunting up lace for "stock", in 1891, was found to have hoarded up in a box 15s. worth of lace, and was diligently working to add to her store, hoping some day to be able to sell it. When our visitor bought the boxful as it was the tears of joy came into her eyes. She is now eighty-seven years of age, and is still making lace.

In almost every village something was done. There was want of method, perhaps, and waste of force, but it was an enthusiasm; no one believed at the time that there was any great business possibility in the lace industry. An attempt to bring order into the chaos resulted in the formation of the "Midland Lace Association". A letter which appeared in the *Northampton Daily Chronicle* for January 12th, 1897, explains the genesis of this Association:—

"LACE ASSOCIATION FOR THE COUNTIES OF NORTHAMPTON, BUCKINGHAM, AND BEDFORD: A SHORT ACCOUNT OF ITS ORIGIN AND FORMATION

"On February 3rd, 1891, an exhibition of needlework and pillow lace was held in Northampton, and was opened by H.R.H. the Duchess of Teck. There were 550 exhibits of pillow lace, all made in the above counties. A large amount of prizes was awarded to the poor lace-workers; indeed, so great was the interest exhibited, and so large the quantity of lace sold, that it seemed a pity to let the industry die out (as it was fast doing) for want of encouragement. A preliminary meeting was held in St. Giles's Vicarage, and the scheme of the Lace Association was drawn up. The Countess Spencer kindly consented to act as president, with twelve vice- presidents, and five ladies were appointed to act as a working committee. There was also a general committee of subscribers, whose subscriptions enabled the working committee to buy in a stock of lace, and to meet the expenses of postage, printing, etc.

"The objects of the Association were—

"1. To stimulate and improve the local manufacture of lace.

"2. To provide workers with greater facilities for the sale of their work at more remunerative prices.

"3. To provide instruction in lace-making.

"Wherever it was possible a lady correspondent was appointed to act as a medium of communication between the lace-workers and the committee.

"At first the lace was sold through the agency of a depôt in Northampton, but at the end of six months the working committee took upon themselves the whole responsibility of the sales, and with so much success that the amount of lace sold has gone on steadily increasing each year, and so great now is the demand for this beautiful fabric that the committee find it difficult to keep pace with the orders that flow in.

"In consequence of the great demand for lace the work of the Association has increased to such an extent that it has been found necessary this year to appoint a special agent to buy and sell for the committee. It is hoped in time (if the demand for lace goes on increasing) that the Association will become self-supporting; but at present, owing to the increased expenses connected with its working, it is still more or less dependent upon subscriptions. I must not omit to add that in 1894 the Lace Association was honoured by an order for 360 yards of pillow lace by H.R.H. the Duchess of York. Before concluding this little sketch it is only right to mention that before the Lace Association was even thought of, ladies in Northamptonshire and the adjoining counties had endeavoured to revive the industry in their own immediate neighbourhoods. Mrs. Chettle, who is now an active member of the Lace Association, began her work in 1888, and before the Association was started had sold £200 worth of lace. Miss M. Roberts, of Spratton, in 1890, started a small subscription fund to enable her to buy the poor people's lace, which she sold for them amongst her friends. So far back as 1880 Mrs Harrison, of Paulers Pury, began to take an interest in it. She sold a large quantity of lace to the Ladies' Work Society in Sloane Street, and in 1883 received an order from H.R.H. the Princess Louise and the Duchess of Edinburgh. In 1883 she furnished the Princess Christian, by special request, with notes and statistics of the Bucks lace industry for an article H.R.H. was writing in *Murray's Magazine*, and this article brought the lace-makers into notice, and furnished them with fresh orders. In 1891 Mrs. Harrison joined the Lace Association, and took an active interest in the formation of County Council lace-classes for the various villages of Northamptonshire...

"Miss Dryden's able and interesting article in the *Pall Mall Magazine* of March last brought the lace into further notice, and has also been the means of bringing in fresh orders, amongst others one from a Russian nobleman, who sent a donation to the Association, and also asked for patterns and parchments of English-made pillow laces for his mother, who is a 'past master' in the art of Russian pillow lace-making, and who wishes to copy some of our English-made laces. In conclusion I would add that I received an 'award' from Chicago for specimens of pillow lace sent on behalf of the Midland lace-makers.

"GEORGINA M. ROBERTS.

"SPRATTON VICARAGE, NORTHAMPTON."

Mrs. Roberts, the writer of this letter, is herself a most accomplished lace-maker, familiar with the methods of the old Italian laces, of the Honiton lace, of the heavy linen laces, as well as being a good point-ground worker. The Association beginning as it did, with far too little capital (only £15), was unable by itself to carry on a business which developed so rapidly as did the pillow-lace trade. The ladies of the working committee, therefore, dipped generously into their own pockets, and added largely to the capital without seeking for any return in the form of interest or profit. This generous spending did not appear in the accounts of the Lace Association, that business being kept separate from the further individual efforts of the ladies, though all worked harmoniously together for its good. Through stress of circumstances and from convenience, and partly on account of Mrs. Roberts's nearness to Northampton, the work of the Association proper fell mainly into her hands. She bought and sold lace and thread and parchments, superintending as no ordinary secretary could have done, carrying on for *no* pecuniary reward a business which filled the whole of the working-day with arduous labour. It must be remembered that lace teachers and prickers were almost extinct, that good thread and pins were difficult to obtain, that many of the younger lacemakers had been trained in bad methods. Mrs. Roberts experimented with threads and patterns; there was no lace which she did not understand and could not correct. Wisely comprehending that success could not attend mere lifeless revivals of old work, she collected patterns and laces from all over Europe, and welcomed every kind of work that was good. In 1897 she was obliged to give up the work of selling and buying, and it was placed in the hands of a lady agent in Northampton, who has carried it on with untiring devotion.

Another member of the first working committee was Mrs. Chettle, who is referred to in Mrs. Roberts's letter. This lady found distress among the population about Towcester in 1865, on account of slackness in the shoe trade, and she then helped the people by disposing of £200 worth of lace amongst her friends. Afterwards she allowed her interest in lace-making to drop until the year 1888, when she began to devote herself to the task of buying and selling, and now has a large connection. Mrs. Bostock, who bought and sold in the town of Northampton, also belonged to the first committee.

At Prince's Risborough Mrs. Forrest carried on the same work, and many others laboured, following the example of the originators of the movement. Mrs. Harrison of Paulers Pury was one of the first to carry on lace-buying on a large scale, though she did not join the Association till 1891.

All these ladies took the place of the old professional lace-buyers, who had almost all given up the trade in the time of its decline. They began, generally in a small way, to buy the lace of old workers out of charity and also from the pure love of it. The rapidity with which these small beginnings became, in the hands of ladies unaccustomed to business and with no wish to make money, large affairs in which the annual expenditure amounted to hundreds of pounds, shows the real vitality of the trade; it shows that at any rate it was not dead because it was not wanted. All who entered into it were carried along, as it were, involuntarily devoting their lives and their money without any previous planning, plunging suddenly into important business transactions just because they happened to be on the spot to do the work and there was no one else to do it. There have been no great losses, neither has there been much profit, for the lace has generally been sold at very little over cost price. It has not been possible, however, to work the Association as distinct from the individual work of the ladies (though it has been only financially distinct) without expenses; it has therefore been to a small extent in debt.

VIII

THE CONDITION AND PROSPECTS OF
LACE-MAKING AT THE PRESENT TIME

HAS the industry a future? is it business or is it charity? No question is more often put to the modern lady lace-buyer. There is a great demand, so great that, it must be frankly confessed, it very often cannot be met. Sometimes orders have to be refused, often orders which could be had for the asking are not asked for. Lace-buyers, both the amateur (who has by far the greater part of the business) and the genuine trader working for his own profit, constantly reiterate the cry, "I could sell if I could get the work." It is workers we want, workers by the hundred, workers who will make the *kind of lace we need*. There are some lace-makers who will offer to make you any kind of lace except the one which you happen to want at the moment. Generally you are forced to buy anything they will consent to make on account of the necessity of keeping up your stock, though it may be almost impossible to get a profit on that particular work.

This state of things very naturally suggests the question. Is the work needed, or are we so rich that we can do without such an industry? There is undoubtedly a considerable class of persons to whom it is an immense boon, to whom its disappearance would be an irreparable loss. There are hundreds of women between sixty and ninety years of age quite unfit for any other kind of work who keep themselves by it in independence; any lace-buyer can count up a large number who keep their husbands as well—husbands past work, crippled, or blind, or bedridden. The old mother living in the son's or daughters house, past being any assistance in the housework, feels the delight of not being a burden on the hard-pressed children. She can still sit at her pillow part of the day and earn the four or five shillings a week which keeps her. Perhaps to the aged the occupation is almost as great a boon as the earnings, and this accounts for the intense pleasure with which the work is almost always spoken of. When sons and daughters are all grown up and gone away, the long days may be unspeakably dull to the old couple, but the wife can always make herself happy turning over the bobbins. We went to see a widow, over eighty years old, living all alone, and tried to buy some of her beautiful lace. "When my husband was alive," she said, "he didn't care for me working at it, so I put it on one side; but now he's dead, I couldn't do without it, I should be so dull." She could not sell us any of her work, she had orders that would keep her busy for months to come.

But it is not only the aged who are glad of the work; the mother of the family finds it a great help. When the housework is done, and the children are all away at school, she can sit down and work for a couple of hours, and the week's earnings will be a comfortable addition to her man's wages, especially when there is a large family and he a labourer on 12s or 14s. a week. There is no other industry so convenient for the home. It is clean work and needs cleanliness, for lace must be spotlessly white if the worker is to get her full price. It creates no litter and no untidiness. The pillow stands by the window, with a cloth thrown over it and the chair ready before it. When baby is put to sleep, the mother has but to lift the cloth and begin her work: there is no getting out of material and implements, and no putting away and clearing up when the children come home to tea. Where shoe-work or stay-work is taken at home, the littered floor and whirring machine make an unpleasant contrast to the tidiness and quietness of the bobbins with their little subdued rattle so pleasant to the ear. Lace-making is not tiring, nor in any way trying; given suitable spectacles for the old women, it is not at all trying to the eyes—indeed, an expert worker on a lace she knows well, looks at it no more than a needlewoman looks at a long seam. "I could do it with my eyes shut" is a phrase one often hears of lace-making, but we take that statement for what it is worth. It is not monotonous work, for even in the simplest lace the pattern creates a variety of motion and sufficient occupation for the mind. "My mother always said that to sit down to her pillow was the best rest she could have after her work," we have been told by the daughter of a famous lace-maker.

On the advantages and pleasures of the work much more might justly be said; but there is one drawback, a drawback that in these days seems to have remarkable force: it takes, in comparison with other home industries, a long time to learn. No one loves shoe-work and stay-work, but they can be learnt with astonishingly little expenditure of time and trouble, and herein lies their superiority. An average woman working in her odd hours cannot earn more than 2s. or 3s. a week until she has been learning lace-making for a year; she may earn as much as that after six months; she will probably earn enough to pay for her pillow and bobbins and material after six weeks. A really first-class lace-maker needs four or five years of training. She is, of course, earning something all the time, and she is not having lessons continuously, but only when she changes from one pattern to another. During the first few weeks, before the fingers become supple and accustomed to the action, the work may seem slow and tedious, and some perseverance is necessary. Unfortunately perseverance is a rare virtue among our villagers; their faint-heartedness in every matter which does not immediately go well is very remarkable, and would be almost beyond belief.

In the old days children began very young; and a child of five or six, who has an opportunity of learning, will often think lace-making a most delightful occupation—superior to all Kindergarten games. But nowadays it cannot be taught until schooldays are over, when the girls get out of the regular school routine, and are unsettled and disinclined to steady work. Then, after a little loafing about at home, they are off to service, and we wonder where the next generation of lace-makers is to come from. If the babies could be taught to handle the bobbins in schooltime, instead of plaiting paper mats (no easier to do) and other Kindergarten occupations, and if the girls in the upper school could have an hour or two a week for lace-making instead of working thousands of sums which do not lead to any comprehension of mathematics, and are never likely to be of the smallest use to them, they would, when they leave school, be fairly efficient lace-makers. This need not in anywise prevent their going to service, but in the interval of looking out for a good place they would be useful members of society; they would have a valuable resource in a case of breakdown of health, and after their marriage they would have a pleasant and refining occupation for spare hours. If money is not greatly needed, lace can be made for baby's clothes. The first piece of lace made to trim the little daughter's pinafore has been a great source of pride and pleasure to a married lace pupil. Unless we can train young lace-makers

now, the trade must pass away with the present generation. All our
present workers (the exceptions are too few to be taken into account)
were trained in lace schools; they paid a little for learning, and got their
earnings meanwhile. The system was admirably adapted to the nature
of the industry it provided; it provided an economical system of
excellent technical training without the help of rates or Government
grant. To commence such a period of teaching now after the girls leave
school is out of the question. Even putting on one side the need of
domestic servants, they could not, after thirteen years of age, be kept
training for three or four years for a profession, when they should be
keeping themselves. The economy of the old system lay in the fact that
a girl, beginning quite young, could do very well by the time she was
thirteen or fourteen. Something is, however, being done. In some
villages a class is held once or twice a week after school hours, to which
girls over eleven years old come. The classes generally include some
who have already left school, but who are waiting to be old enough to
go into good service. Unfortunately it is an expensive matter to keep
such classes going for any length of time, as the girls seldom care to pay
for their instruction. They expect to learn everything for nothing,
because the elementary schools are free; also they do not feel
sufficiently sure of being able to continue their work to care to spend
money upon it. A lace school of this kind has been started by Mrs.
Guthrie at East Haddon, Northamptonshire [*Fig. 14*]. She provides a
teacher for girls twice a week in a sort of parish room in the village.
Here also, on one day in the week, the writer holds a class for adults. In
connection with the school is an industry for the production of fine
lace-trimmed household linen. It is hoped to be able to rival the
wonderfully dainty linen goods of Austria and Germany; and, indeed,
there seems to be no difficulty in doing so, for the only complaint
made of our towels by a Bond Street shop was that they were *too*
beautiful; ladies would not buy them for the purpose for which they
were intended. Yet there was no unsuitability of material; it was
merely a matter of dainty needlework and perfectly harmonious
design. Ladies do our drawn-thread work, and we make a point of
suiting the stitch and linen to the lace. In this matter of harmony and
oneness of design the beautiful foreign linen is often a failure. There is
no doubt about our being able to do it, but we need more workers. East

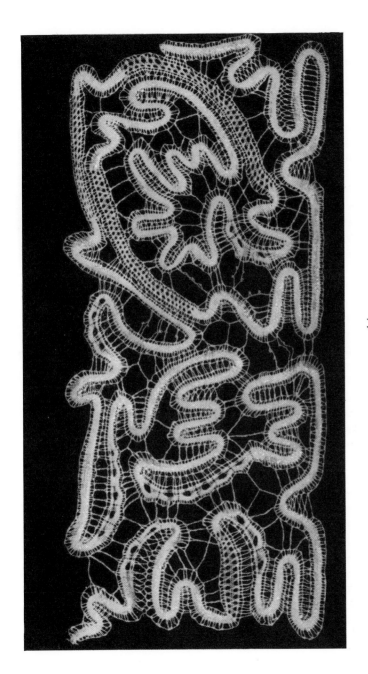

FIG. 14

MODERN PILLOW LACE

MADE AT EAST HADDON AFTER OLD ITALIAN STYLE

Haddon is not the only village where these classes are held. On bicycle or horseback Miss Channer goes from one to another, holding more than one class a day in villages three or four miles apart.

County Councils give but a meagre help in this great question of the technical training of the lace-maker. The Northampton County Council gives this year £15 for lace-making. One village may claim £3, which will keep a class going for about six weeks. At the end of that time, if no generous patron is ready to pay for its continuance, the girls probably give up trying, and all the time and money is wasted.

At Paulers Pury Mrs. Harrison persuades many mothers to teach their daughters. But Paulers Pury is an exceptional place; it has excellent traditions; its point-ground laces are unrivalled; there is an abundance of good patterns—in fact, patterns which do not take prizes at lace competitions are usually eliminated. Here, as many as one in three of the female population are lace-makers. In other parts of the counties a much smaller proportion of the mothers are lace-makers, and a still smaller proportion are *good* lace-makers. Many mothers cannot, and many will not take the trouble, to teach their daughters.

In Mrs. Guthrie's school linen laces, both of the German and Italian style, are taught as well as the fine point-ground edgings [*Fig. 15*]. At one of Miss Channer's classes held at Spratton real Valenciennes is being taught. The people are quick and ready to learn a new lace if only the teaching problem can be dealt with; this problem is successfully solved abroad and is undoubtedly the foundation of foreign lace-making. It is true that we cannot compete with foreigners in the production of cheap torchon lace. Our people will not work for so little money as the Swiss and Germans and Belgians.

After dealing with country lace-makers one wonders how, even in towns, "sweating" can be possible in England! One longs for some of the poor hard-worked Londoners to help build up our trade. When our villagers refuse to make lace as cheaply as it is imported from abroad, it must be remembered that the foreign work is generally inferior. It is surely a matter for some honest pride that most of our women would be ashamed to ask us to buy lace such as one sees in some London shop windows; they take a pride in their work, and will not often lower its quality for more gain. "Look into it and you'll see it's good work", says a woman standing out for what she considers a fair price. "I would

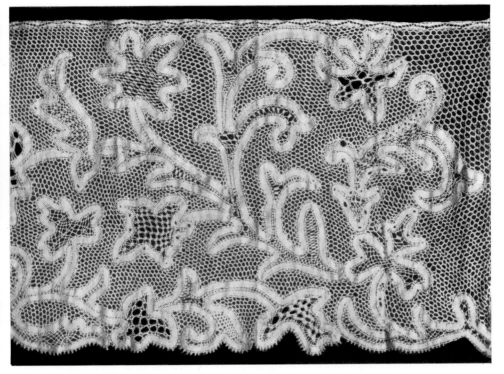

not show it you at all if you could not say it is well made." Yet that woman was dependent on lace to keep her and her blind husband from abject poverty; her pride would not have allowed her to take a penny off the price, nor to offer anything but the best work. The public does not always distinguish between good and bad quality; it asks for something cheap. It sees in a shop window "Real Torchon, 2*d*.," and it says, "How wonderfully cheap! I'll have a dozen yards." The Northamptonshire woman would have remarked, "I would not be a foreigner to make such stuff," and she would have been taunted with the reproach, "You can't do it so cheap." No, we cannot, and we do not succeed when we try to be cheap. There is a certain knack in turning out poor work of a perfectly uniform quality. The writer has deliberately tried to imitate poor Brussels lace, but she can only make it hopelessly and unevenly bad, or uniformly good and expensive. English people must triumph by the superiority of their work if they are to triumph at all, and if it is good they must be well paid for it. It is in the best and most expensive laces that we must try to make our way, leaving two-penny torchon to the foreigner. It is unfortunate that our British public has an hereditary preference for expensive foreign lace over British. Many a lady will take pleasure in spending £10 on lace in Venice when she will hesitate to spend 10s. on equally good lace in Northampton! It is uninteresting and unromantic to buy lace in Northampton, even if it is exactly like the Venetian and no more expensive.

Having dealt at some length with the condition of the industry as regards the worker, we must, before passing on to other aspects, show what are the earnings of a lace-maker. There are a few women who get £1 per week or more; many more could earn as much if they could be properly taught. The average among those who devote a considerable amount of time to it is perhaps 10s. per week. Some will only earn 5s., and some very old women not more than 2s. or 3s. There are hardly any women who really give up all their time to it; very few who sit at it regularly many hours a day. To earn one's shilling a day *after* the housework and cooking is done is considered a very creditable performance. These earnings ought not to be compared with those of girls working regularly in factories; for there cannot be the steady uninterrupted work at home, where four or five hours is a good measure, in addition to other duties and interruptions. How does the industry stand from the trader's point of view? This is a much-debated question.

At the time when the trade was at its lowest ebb, ten or twelve years ago, almost all the professional lace-buyers had abandoned it. Mr. Smith, at Olney, tells us that he continued merely from love of the work without hope of profit. The profits are still extremely small, but he, like everyone else, complains of having too small a staff of workers. Mr. W. Robinson, of Bedford, turned his attention to millinery laces of horsehair and fibre; they are worked on old yak and torchon parchments, but some of them resemble straw plaiting more than lace. The field then was absolutely free for the amateur; there was practically no competition with the lace-buyers. The situation was a unique one; ladies who were amateurs in the art of buying and selling found themselves masters of a rising industry, which in its former flourishing days had always been carried on from the strictly commercial point of view; nor can there have been many other trades in England so entirely in the hands of women.

It would have been surprising indeed if no mistakes had been made; it is surprising that so few were made. Time has proved that it was a mistake to begin the Lace Association with so small a capital; taking the individual lace business of the various ladies, those who have put the most money into it have the most flourishing industry and have suffered the least loss.

At present an attempt is being made to start the Midland Lace Association on a new basis with a solid capital, on which interest can be paid if the present conditions continue. An offshoot of this association, the North Bucks Lace Association, which remains affiliated to the parent society, has begun in a business-like way, having the advantage that always comes of beginning later and profiting by the mistakes of one's predecessors. It is excellently organised and does good work.

Another mistake was that of keeping prices too low. The women for a few years had had great difficulty in selling their lace and expected to get very little for it; they therefore accepted absurdly little remuneration for their work. The new buyers, not wishing to make any profit, sold it again for very little. This was a drawback in many ways. First of all it kept young people from wishing to learn lace-making; so little could be earned, that only old lace-makers who could do very little else, cared to take it up, and buyers were dependent upon a generation which was passing away. In the second place, no one who desired to make a profit could begin trading in lace, as they would inevitably be undersold by the ladies. The consequence, if this had continued, would have been that a very large body of workers would have been dependent upon the existence of a sufficiently large body of ladies willing to work very hard at this trade for nothing, a state of things which could not be guaranteed to last

Another way in which low prices have been a hindrance, has been the difficulty of supplying shops, who would have been good customers. The shop could not put on its fair profit and sell the lace, when it could be had for so very much less by writing to a Northamptonshire lady, or at one of the lace sales and exhibitions. The Association, which could not sell as economically as ladies could sell among their own friends, was to a certain extent undersold. It could not make even a large enough profit to pay the expenses of keeping up an Association shop, which would undoubtedly have been an advantage to the industry. Fortunately this condition of things is now righting itself. Prices are gradually rising, though some good laces are still being sold for too little, which may soon have the effect of making them disappear from the market. Ladies in connection with the Association have agreed to add a definite percentage to the cost price of their lace. The need of a larger staff of workers has to some extent forced up the scale of remuneration to the lace-maker, though if this had happened sooner we should to-day be in a better position and able to put a larger stock into the market. With better prices, lace shops are buying, to a much larger extent than formerly, from Midland villages; but the bulk of the trade is still in the hands of the Association and those connected with it. With good management this may easily remain so, for we are more popular with the lace-makers than is the commercial traveller, and we get all the best work. When they are well served, the shops are very willing to trade with us, and we can often send them a better selection than their own travellers can obtain. Personal experience would suggest that shop managers are the *most* satisfactory persons to deal with, for they are invariably courteous and business-like, and withal pay promptly, which cannot always be said of our lady customers. We should not be always in such need of capital if we could avoid bad debts; the necessity of paying workers immediately makes it very trying to be obliged to wait months and months for the price of lace sold, and means much drawing upon the lace banking account.

A good idea of the stock which we can show could have been gathered at the lace exhibition and sale held by kind permission of the Earl and Countess Spencer at Spencer House on July 12th of last year. The value of the lace in the room was calculated at about £800. Probably not much of what was unsold that day remained many weeks on hand. It represents pretty accurately what the Association can produce at short notice, but it does not give a correct idea of the whole output of the three counties. It did not include the work of the North

Bucks Association, which held a separate and very successful sale, nor does it show the great quantity of lace made to order on which workers are continually engaged. These periodical sales are at present necessary to bring the customers into touch with the work, but it would be to the convenience of the customer and to the advantage of the trade if this stock could be shown at a permanent shop or depôt.

The existence of an industry is not entirely a question of supply and demand; opportunity and organisation are important factors. In our three lace counties we have a body of expert lace-makers capable of holding their own against any foreign manufacturers, if they are given a chance, if the trade can be organised on lines favourable to its development. We have tried to show that its life or death is very largely a question of technical education, yet all that has been done for the training of the lace-maker is owing to private generosity. The County Councils help with the merest pittance, and neutralise the little good they do by imposing oppressive regulations.

A teacher now working under the Northampton County Council is told that she cannot be paid for her work until four other villages have finished their courses of lessons. She does not know whether these villages have even begun. Besides being asked to wait for her remuneration for an indefinite period, she has to *advance money herself* for pillows, bobbins, and threads, for the same reason that no money can be paid to her until the other four villages of which she knows nothing have finished their work. Not many teachers would consent to such conditions. Such a system may answer for technical classes, like those held for teaching wood-carving, which are merely for improving amusement, but for a serious trade it is an absurdity. The supineness of the authorities of the counties concerned is extraordinary. Lace-making cannot be learnt at the Technical School in Northampton, nor is design taught with any view to its being utilised for lace-making. In spite of the number of curious relics of the past in the shape of lace-pillows, pins, winders, candle-blocks, flasks, bobbins, dicky-pots, maids, etc., which abound in the county, the Northampton museum only shows one dirty, neglected pillow and horse. There is no collection of old parchments, no collection of lace (though a collection of Northampton lace would be of supreme interest), and no collection of lace designs and draughts for the county.

Literature on the subject of lace-making is unattainable at the Northampton Public Library; we have tried in vain to hear in Northampton of one single book on the subject of lace. We have depended upon the kindness of friends having valuable books in their possession, and of Mr. Alan Cole, of the South Kensington Museum, in allowing us to make use of his splendid lecture on the art of lace-making. South Kensington is generous in allowing us to make use of photographs, and in the museum every facility is given for the study of the splendid collection of lace, but in the counties themselves no help can be obtained by the novice in lace. We have been starved and snubbed and neglected, and then we are told the industry is not wanted because it has not been a great success! If only one little room could be found in Northampton for a good lace museum; if only a few standard books could be provided; if design, and the pricking and preparing of lace parchments could be taught in the technical school, what an improvement there would be!

The writers of this little book have turned their attention to the preparation of parchments. Miss M. Roberts, after studying the "principles of design" under Mr. Knight at the Technical School, Northampton, has tried by herself to apply her knowledge and skill to lace design, and with considerable success [*Fig. 16*]. She is now prepared to produce suitable patterns for all kinds of lace for any kind of purpose. Miss Channer has experimented in the pricking of parchments with a view to discovering the best method to teach others, in order that pricking may not continue to be, as it now is in England, a lost art. The so-called "prickers" who remain depend entirely upon old parchments for the pricking of a point ground; they are incapable of ruling out any pattern for themselves. The old methods can be studied in the remarkable draughts in the possession of Mr. Smith, lace-buyer, of Olney.

Surely the existence in our midst of such beautiful art and handicraft as that of lace-making is worth an effort, worth some public attention, some public expenditure. It is natural to our people; it is absolutely at home in our three counties; it is beloved by thousands of our villagers, mixed with all the romance of their lives, a blessing to the old and the delight of the young. One notes the little girls' delight to use an old bobbin with "grandfather's name on it" as one teaches in a class of to-

FIG. 16

DESIGN FOR LACE FAN BY MISS ROBERTS

day, and one's mind wanders back in imagination to the days when grandmother was young and had husband's and children's names on her pillow, when the little ones were sent off day by day to the lace school, when the young man gave his sweetheart pretty beaded bone bobbins to make her pillow smart, and the old man stayed at home to make lace, and it seems as if all the romance and interest of life centred round the curious old bundle of straw, "my pillow". We must take it to heart that the words are not a mere relic of the past, but a living factor in thousands of homes to-day.

LACE MAKING IN THE THREE
LACE COUNTIES FROM 1900

By Anne Buck

THE LACE ASSOCIATIONS 1900-1930

WHEN Miss Channer and Miss Roberts were writing *Lace-making in the Midlands* the decline of the trade had reduced the number of lace dealers and the buying and selling of lace was passing into different hands (p. 81). Women of the rectories and vicarages of the lacemaking district, including the mother of Miss Roberts, and some of the local gentry organised the sale of village lace.

Mrs Harrison, wife of the rector of Paulerspury came there on her marriage in the 1880s and took up this responsibility with energy and enthusiasm. Paulerspury, a village south of Towcester on the Buckinghamshire border, had been noted for its fine point ground lace and had its own resident lacebuyer, Edward Rose, who had died just before Mrs Harrison arrived. She has left her own account, written after 1912, of the hardship caused by the death of Mr Rose because the village lost the main outlet for its lace and also lost the source of its patterns. Mrs Harrison discovered that Mr Rose's widow still lived in the village and had many of her husband's parchments which, according to custom, had always been returned to him with the finished lace. The lacemakers feared that Mrs Rose who had 'never been partial to lacemaking' would destroy these parchments. Mrs Harrison visited her and was told she could have them for 5s, 'and a good riddance', so fearing a change of mind, she at once 'gathered them up in my skirt (we wore long dresses in those days) and carried them home to my husband rejoicing'.

Elizabeth Rose of Paulerspury had exhibited lace at the Great Exhibition of 1851. She was probably the Mrs E. Rose who appears as lacebuyer, Paulerspury, in a local directory of 1854, succeeded by Edward Rose in later directories of 1864 and 1877. From Mrs Harrison's account this was not likely to have been the surviving Mrs Rose and was probably Edward Rose's mother. Mrs Harrison

organised the sale of lace made in the village amongst her friends and through the Ladies' Work Society in London, so that once again the workers had a market and Mr Rose's patterns to work from. There were still skilled lacemakers in Paulerspury and very fine lace continued to be made there (*Pls 5 & 6*). Mrs Harrison mentions others who supported the industry in the district by financing and organising village work, Mrs Chettle of Potterspury, Miss Wake of Courtenhall, Mrs Wilson of Preston Deanery, Miss Dryden of Canons Ashby and Lady Knightley of Fawsley and 'also Miss Channer who when quite a young girl wrote a very comprehensive little book on "Lace-making in the Midlands" and who now has a lace school in Abingdon [sic] St Northampton'. As Miss Channer and Miss Roberts wrote of this time, 'In almost every village something was done. There was want of method, perhaps, and waste of force, but it was enthusiasm' (p. 68).

The Midland Lace Association.   In 1891 the Home Arts and Industries Association, formed in the 1880s to organise classes in domestic crafts, held an exhibition in Northampton which included a display of lace, bringing these separate village achievements together. This led to the formation, later in the year, of the first of the Lace Associations, The Midland Lace Association with Mrs Harrison and Mrs Roberts on its small working committee. In a letter written to the Daily Chronicle quoted in full by Miss Channer and Miss Roberts (pp. 69-70) Mrs Roberts gives her first-hand account of the founding of the Midland Association.

Ladies of the nobility and gentry, who may have cared little for lacemaking as a local industry, did react to the effect its decline had on the elderly women who still depended on it for a living. They saw the Lace Associations as a philanthropic activity worthy of support. Their annual subscriptions provided initial capital, and in part the yearly income, needed to pay for lace, yard by yard, while it was still on the pillow. Lacemakers could not afford to wait for

PLATE 5. (On preceding page) Flounce worked at Paulerspury, Northants, 1900-10. This may have been worked from one of the older parchments left by Mr E. Rose, who was a lace dealer in Paulerspury in the 1860s and 1870s. Slightly reduced; actual width 250 mm. (*Northampton Museum*)

PLATE 6. Two Paulerspury lacemakers, 1900–10; the one on the right has the lace of Plate 5 on her pillow. (*Northampton Museum*)

payment long enough to work a saleable length of the better quality laces and so had turned to the cheaper laces with their quicker but smaller return. The ultimate aim was that sales of lace should make the Associations increasingly self-supporting. Mrs Roberts was the active force in the organisation and the work of the Midland Association 'fell mainly into her hands' until 1897 (p. 71).

The Buckinghamshire Lace Association. By this time a second association was being formed in Buckinghamshire where the same enthusiasm had been at work. Miss Rose Hubbard organised the Winslow Lace Industry there in the 1870s, and in the 1890s Miss Burrows of Maids Moreton near Buckingham gave the name Buckinghamshire Lace Industry to her group of workers. The new association, the North Buckinghamshire Lace Association was affiliated to the Midland Association.

An Association for Bedfordshire Lacemaking. In 1904 steps were taken to form an association for Bedfordshire lacemaking, but Bedfordshire and North Buckinghamshire combined under the new name Buckinghamshire Lace Association (North Bucks and Bedfordshire) with an impressive list of royal patrons and titled vice-presidents. It was able to start on a sounder financial basis than the pioneer Midland Association.

The aims of all the Associations were to sell lace from maker direct to buyer, cutting out the profit made by middlemen, so that lacemakers could get a better price for their work; to encourage the making of better quality lace, particularly the point ground traditional in the East Midlands before 1850; and to organise classes in lacemaking so that a new generation could carry on the industry and the tradition. In practice they were taking the place of lacebuyers, marketing the lace and supplying thread and patterns; with the additional aim of teaching lacemaking.

The Associations were not charities, for the lacemakers earned every penny they received, but they were run as charitable organisations from country drawing rooms by women in positions of social dominance. Social dominance imposed its own limitations on the activities of individuals, especially if those individuals were women. It was the philanthropic aim of the Associations on behalf of the lacemakers which made voluntary work for them normal and acceptable. Patronage of the lace itself, a decorative fabric of beauty and delicacy gave an artistic edge to the philanthropic aim, for it implied that those involved had the discernment to distinguish handmade lace from the machine work which was taking over much of the market.

The running of the Associations depended on a few active, enthusiastic members who were generous with their time and energy and sometimes financial support. Few though had Mrs Roberts's lacemaking skills or Miss Channer's grasp of lacemaking as an industry. In 1911 the Midland Association's income from subscriptions was £30 2s 6d (*Pl. 7*). There were nineteen "patronesses" but not all of these appear on the list of subscribers. There was a committee of twenty-four members, with a smaller working committee of nine members. The Association made a profit for the year of £25 0s 9d on sales of lace. At first run entirely by voluntary workers, it now had a paid collector. When Miss Channer acted as their agent at the Northampton headquarters at 8a George Row, in 1912, she was paid £4 11s 8d per month. By 1914 this had risen to £6 and in 1918 to £8. By then Miss Channer had been succeeded by Miss McAuslin as agent.

The headquarters of the Midland Association remained in Northampton. A Midland Lace Association shop is listed in local directories until 1931. The Buckinghamshire Association was able to set up a London depot for the sale of lace. Both Associations held exhibitions and sales of work, the Midland Association an annual exhibition in Northampton, the Buckinghamshire Association from time to time a London one. Exhibitions and sales continued, though with lessening support, into the 1920s.

To help the women still making lace and needing income from it, the Associations concentrated first on marketing, supplying linen thread (*Pl. 8*) and patterns for fine quality lace which they could sell and wanted to encourage. Taking over the retailing of lace and selling through voluntary workers they made no allowance for normal distribution costs. This undermined the marketing of

The Midland Counties Lace Association.

TRADING ACCOUNT.

January 1st, 1911, to December 30th, 1911.

	£ s. d.		£ s. d.
Jan. 1/11—To Stock... ... ...315 14 11		Dec. 30/11—By Sales 760 12 5	
Dec. 30/11—To Purchases 564 17 5½		Dec. 30/11—By Stock-in-Trade ...233 6 3	
Dec. 30/11—To Gross Profit, c/d. 113 6 3½			
	£993 18 8		£993 18 8

PROFIT AND LOSS ACCOUNT.

January 1st, 1911 to December 30th, 1911.

	£ s. d.	£ s. d.		£ s. d.
To Salary	55 0 0		By Gross Profit 113 6 3½	
„ Commission, 1911	9 4 2		„ Subscriptions 30 2 6	
		64 4 2	„ Bank Interest 4 6 6	
„ Rent		... 16 0 0	„ Profit of Tea Stall 2 5 6	
„ General Expenses ...		... 28 3 7		
„ Postages, Stationery, etc.		... 16 12 3½		
„ Net Profit to Capital Account		25 0 9		
		£150 0 9½		£150 0 9½

BALANCE SHEET.

December 30th, 1911.

LIABILITIES.	£ s. d.	ASSETS.	£ s. d.
To Creditors for Commission, Expenses, etc. 18 6 3		By Northants Union Bank, Ltd. ... 490 10 10	
„ Capital Account 711 3 10		„ By Cash in Hand 3 15 0	
		„ Subscriptions Outstanding ... 1 18 0	
		„ Stock-in-Trade 233 6 3	
	£729 10 1		£729 10 1

We have examined the above Balance Sheet, and in our opinion same correctly sets forth the financial position of the Association at date thereof.

We have received a Certificate to the effect that the Stock-in-Trade has been taken at Cost Prices or under.

A. C. PALMER & CO.,
Chartered Accountants and Auditors.

St. Giles' Chambers, Northampton,
March 16th, 1912.

Plate 7. Report of the Midland Counties Lace Association for 1911 showing the amount of lace bought and sold. (*Northampton Record Office, X4542*)

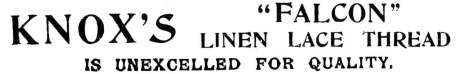

KNOX'S "FALCON" LINEN LACE THREAD
IS UNEXCELLED FOR QUALITY.

Sold in Skeins and on 100 and 200-yard Spools.

Please compare LACE MADE FROM LINEN THREAD with Cotton Lace.

Linen Lace wears a lifetime and KEEPS ITS COLOUR

There is nothing better than the best.

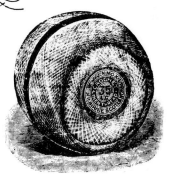

KNOX'S "L.C."
LINEN CROCHET THREAD

Made up 12 Balls per Box.
Also in Skeins and Spools.

Very suitable for all descriptions of Crochet Work.   Try a sample Ball.

 Cheapness is not based on what you pay,
But on what you get for what you pay.

STOCKED BY
THE MIDLAND LACE ASSOCIATION,
8a GEORGE ROW
NORTHAMPTON

Y 1

PLATE 8. Advertisement for the linen thread recommended and stocked by the Midland Lace Association for lacemaking; and showing that they also stocked material for the allied craft of crochet. They had a shop at this address between 1912 and c. 1935. (*Northampton Museum*)

lace through shops which had been accustomed to sell it. The practice of private sales by those who had already built up their own network of customers also hampered the collective effort of each Association. They had some success in getting slightly better prices for the workers and in providing more discerning customers for the finer quality laces.

While Miss Channer was in India teaching lacemaking there, the Associations had built up their market and sources of supply. In the ten years before the outbreak of war in 1914 they achieved their greatest success.

In the first decade of the twentieth century the Buckinghamshire Association reported improvement both in the quality of the lace made and in the demand for it. A catalogue of the North Bucks Lace Association (c.1904) shows that point ground lace of good quality was being made (*Pls 9 & 10*). The Midland Association bought lace valued at £564 17s 5½d during 1911 and their sales of lace for the year realised £760 12s 5d. By August 1922 the sales of lace during the month realised only £25 18s 2½d with the total monthly income which included sales of thread and other equipment, £95 and the total outgoings £94 18s 11d. The fashionable demand, 'an hereditary preference' was still for the lace of Brussels, Mechlin, Valenciennes, Milan or Venice. 'Many a lady will take pleasure in spending £10 on lace in Venice when she will hesitate to spend 10s on equally good lace in Northampton' (p. 80).

By this time lacemakers with experience of working fine point ground patterns were mostly elderly women who often found it difficult to cope with the Associations' demands for lace of a type and quality they had not made for years (*Pls 11 & 12*). During 1910 one lacemaker making lace for the Midland Association generally received 1s a yard, but she also made better quality lace which brought her 19s and 19s 6d a yard, and borders, which were probably for handkerchiefs, at 5s. Her income for the year was £16 10s 6d but the cost of thread would have lessened this to £15 at most. The Associations had acquired many fine patterns of the first half of the nineteenth century but these had often to be adapted and they also needed new patterns in keeping with contemporary

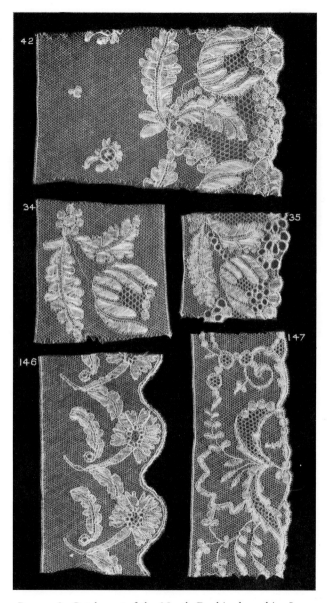

PLATE 9. Catalogue of the North Buckinghamshire Lace Association, c. 1905. The prices per yard of the edgings and insertions shown here are No. 35, *Tulip*, 16s 9d; No. 42, *Tulip*, £2 10s; No. 146, *Carnation*, 14s; No. 147, *Spray*, 10s 6d; No. 34, *Tulip*, 15s 9d. All samples one third actual size.

PLATE 10. Catalogue of the North Buckinghamshire Association, c. 1905. Handkerchief border, *Oak leaf*, price £1 9s 9d; half actual size.

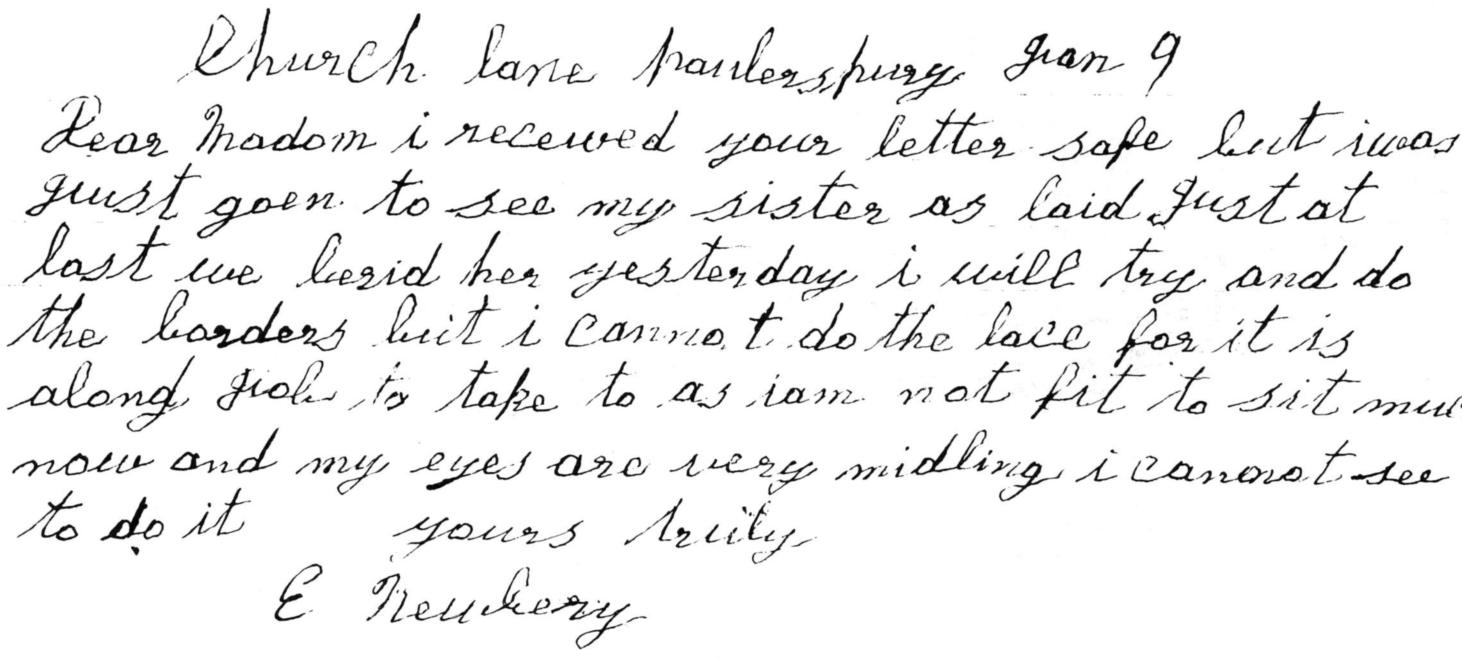

Church. lane Paulerspury Jan 9

Dear Madom i recevied your letter safe but i was just gone. to see my sister as i said just at last we legid her yesterday i will try and do the borders but i cannot. do the lace for it is along job. to take to as i am not fit to suit me i now and my eyes are very midling i cannot see to do it

yours truly

E Newbery

PLATE 11. Letter written to the Midland Lace Association by one of its Paulerspury workers, c. 1912. (*Northamptonshire Record Office*, X4542)

1

Oakhill Farm
forfeild
Hungerford
Berks

Dear maddam
i have sent 2 yards of
Lace if it is of any use to you i am sorrey
to say that i carnt do any more this Winter
as i carnt see to Do it and it upsets me
so i am sorrey to say i have Been in bed
againe very ill but a little better i get
up now but carnt do any Lace yet the
days ar so short for me when i ben do
a little i will try to do you but more
if i shuld Live when the days ar Longer
i shuld be glad if you culd send me
a little more than 15 shillings for it

Dear maddam i have sent you this
thread for you to see how tangle it is
i masted 2 bolts like this i carnt a
forde to by thread to mast Like this we
shall soon have Christmas so i wish you
a mery one and a happy New year
yours Turley m a Lovell
Late of Grendon

PLATE 12. Letter written to the Midland Lace Association from one of its workers, formerly of Grendon, Northamptonshire, c. 1912. Both workers were finding it difficult to work the lace required because of failing sight. (*Northamptonshire Record Office, X4542*)

design. They turned to students of design to provide them but not many students had Miss Roberts's knowledge of lacemaking as well as design training and what they produced could not always be translated into working patterns acceptable to the lacemakers.

THE BEDFORDSHIRE LACE
EDUCATION COMMITTEE 1907-1930

IF HANDMADE lace was to survive as an employment and industry even on a small scale a new generation had to be taught the craft. Miss Channer and Miss Roberts end their book insisting on the importance of technical education, pointing out that there was a missing generation, those who had rejected lacemaking as it declined and had passed on their opposition to it, discouraging their daughters from learning it. The custom of daughters learning from mothers, aunts, or grandmothers survived longer than the lace schools, but that too was gradually dying out and the lace schools had left a legacy of disapproval amongst those in control of education. There was very little demand for instruction in lacemaking from the first generation of universal elementary education after 1870. 'The County Councils help with the merest pittance and neutralise the little good they do by imposing oppressive regulations.' (p. 83). Northamptonshire County Council was then making a grant of £15 a year for classes in the county which had to be held outside school hours and attended only by those above school age. Only the most enthusiastic teacher of lace was likely to hold classes hampered by the financial arrangements described on page 83. The Buckinghamshire Association also received a grant for classes from the County Council after 1911.

Villages had to apply to the county councils to obtain teaching grants. When a village applied to the Bedfordshire County Council in 1906, R.E. Protheroe (later Lord Ernle, a President of the Board of Agriculture) supported the application. In his memoirs, *Whippingham to Westminster* (1938) Lord Ernle tells us what led him to take this action.

'An elderly woman, named Curtis, the wife of the roadman, was a skilled maker of point ground lace. During my tramps through France I had gone out of my way to visit Alenon where in 1880 lace-making was still a cottage industry, and had bought three yards from one of the peasant workers. When I showed this fabric to Mrs. Curtis.... she surprised me by her intelligent comparison of her work with that of her French rival. She told me also that she never had any difficulty in finding customers for her products. The disappearance of such an industry seemed another symptom of the decay of village life. To revive it would be to restore a lost interest, increase earning power, and renew the refining influence of the practice of an artistic craft. For these reasons therefore, in October 1906, I supported an application from a Bedfordshire village for financial assistance in starting a lace class.'

Lord Ernle not only supported this application but proposed that all classes in the county should be the responsibility of the Education Committee.

A sub-committee of the Education Committee, the Bedfordshire Lace Education Sub-Committee, was appointed to administer the county grant and a 'committee of ladies was organised to establish and supervise classes in different parts of the county'. The element of personal and local patronage still lingered as each class was to be under the supervision of 'a lady residing in the district'. A grant of £50 was made for the first year, increased to £75 in 1909 and to £100 in 1911. The increased grant suggests some success during these years. The sole object of this Committee was to establish classes and supply teachers, fine linen thread and good working patterns. It did not undertake the selling of lace. Workers sold through the Associations or to local shops. Classes were held in school buildings outside school hours, for not more than twelve pupils between the ages of nine and sixteen. The Committee provided patterns and all patterns which were not of common design remained Committee property, though others could be sold to workers. A parchment sub-committee was formed in 1913 to acquire and preserve the finer and rarer patterns and to inspect parchments yearly; those too worn to produce good lace were rejected. Work from the classes had to be examined by the Committee; certificates were awarded and exhibitions held.

The initial difficulty was to find teachers for the classes. There were skilled lacemakers in many of the villages but very few had both skill and teaching ability. The few existing teachers of lace either, like Miss Channer, had a natural ability combined with lacemaking skill of the highest order, or were trained teachers who had learned the craft from people like her, or untrained enthusiasts learning with their pupils, for there was no training available. In 1907 teachers were paid 2s 6d a lesson of one and a half to two hours; in 1924 it was 3s. There was no allowance for travelling although the shortage of competent teachers meant that they had to travel from village to village by 'the blessed motor bus' noted in the annual report of 1923; thirty years earlier Miss Channer had travelled on horseback with her pillow strapped to the saddle.

In 1910 and 1911 eighteen classes had been established; this was the maximum number the grant could finance, although there were in addition four to six classes privately financed between 1910 and 1915. The Committee had since 1907 provided the regular financial support for the teaching of lacemaking which had been lacking. But the new lacemakers could not at once supply lace for the high quality market which the Associations were trying to maintain. In 1923 the Committee asked for a grant to train teachers but the policy of the Board of Education was changing. Instruction in lacemaking did not receive much attention in the new policy. As an industry which had exploited its workers it earned disapproval although there were many larger industries, for instance the garment industry, still achieving commercial success with comparable exploitation. It was too small an industry to have a commercial future. As a domestic craft it lacked the practical justification of classes in needlework and cookery for girls and carpentry for boys. Its creative element was not thought sufficient for it to be encouraged in schools of art and design.

Miss. Chalmer
10 a St. Giles Square
Lace School
Northampton

104

PLATE 13. Parchment pattern (lower section), issued by Miss Channer from her school and shop at Northampton, 1915–25. Actual width.

With the opening of new technical schools, grants to voluntary bodies for classes in technical subjects were discontinued. The technical schools were not open to children of elementary school age but lacemaking was to be allowed in the elementary school curriculum in traditional lacemaking areas for one hour a week. Eight schools in the county started these weekly classes in 1925; by 1930 there were only four. The final report of the Bedfordshire Lace Education Committee in 1930 concluded, 'In view of the small number of schools in which it has been found possible to carry out instruction in lacemaking, the lack of teachers and the results obtained, it is doubtful if the continuation in the schools in which it is now taught or its introduction into the Central Schools when they are established is warranted.' The enthusiasm of a teacher at the Harpur Central School, Bedford did, however, mean that it was taught there between 1930 and 1943.

THE END OF AN INDUSTRY, A FUTURE FOR A CRAFT

MISS CHANNER was teaching lacemaking in India when the Bedfordshire Lace Education Sub-Committee was established. Although she continued to live and work in Northamptonshire, working first with the Midland Association, then independently with her own shop and classes in Northampton (*Pl. 13*), she also worked with the Bedfordshire Committee, inspecting classes, judging work shown at exhibitions and advising on parchments. When the Lace Education Committee classes came to an end she took classes at the Bedford Technical Institute for adult education (*Pl. 14*). According to the Institute's prospectus for 1925, 'Buckinghamshire point ground or the coarser Cluny and torshion [sic] form the usual course. Students who desire it may also learn the Honiton, Brussels and Italian laces.' But these were years of declining interest in lace and by 1936 she found that she had to include embroidery with lacemaking to get enough students to make up a class.

106

The Associations were reporting a fall in sales and subscriptions. The war of 1914–18 had given many members a more urgent cause. It also opened a greater choice of employment to women. Domestic service was no longer the only alternative. The Midland Lace Association shop in Northampton closed in the mid 1930s and by the end of the decade all formal organisations had been abandoned.

Some of the parchments collected by the Associations are now in local museums; those of the Midland Association at Northampton and the Buckinghamshire ones at Aylesbury. Parchments stamped 'Bedfordshire Lace Association' are in the Bedford Museum and the Cecil Higgins Art Gallery, Bedford. Some are also stamped with the name of A.A. Carnes who was active in Bedford when the Buckinghamshire and Bedfordshire areas combined in the Buckinghamshire Association. He presented part of his collection to the town when he left Bedford in 1924 and moved to Somerset. He left another group of patterns and photographs to the Somerset County Museum at Taunton. There are others in the Victoria and Albert Museum, London. Some also passed to Miss Haines who carried on the retail side of the Lester lace business in Bedford after 1913, and these are now in Luton Museum. Documents relating to the Midland Lace Association are in Northampton County Record Office; those relating to Buckinghamshire in the Aylesbury Museum; and those of the Bedfordshire Lace Education Committee in the Bedford County Record Office. Lace worked for the Associations can be seen in museums in the East Midlands and some, unrecognised, may have found its way into many other collections. Both patterns and lace show that towards the end of their existence the Associations had dropped their insistence on point ground work.

During her years of retirement at Clapham Miss Channer continued to keep the lacemaking tradition alive. The contribution from that village to the Bedfordshire Women's Institutes' Yearbook for 1949, *Country Crafts, Past and Present*, though anonymous, is unmistakably hers. Her work and influence like that of all teachers, was unspectacular, its effect not recognised until some

107

time had passed. Sadly she did not live to see the skills she had passed on taken up by a new generation. This generation, the lacemakers of the 1960s, with no inherited prejudice against lacemaking came fresh to a new and absorbing craft in social conditions very different from those Miss Channer and Miss Roberts knew in the 1890s.

Miss Channer had shared the enthusiasm for lace and lacemaking which established the Associations but had reservations about their methods of working. She had seen lacemaking as an industry, small, limited perhaps, but to be run as a business organisation. For her it was to become a career, not a philanthropic activity. For a short time, on her return from India she held the post of paid agent for the Midland Association, before detaching herself to set up her own business as maker, designer and teacher of lace. She became a business woman in the lacebuying tradition, making a living and a career in lace. The declining status of English lace, the lack of designers and the decreasing number of skilled workers, had together made this no easy nor profitable undertaking. Miss Channer, like many other women of her generation, was committing herself to changing attitudes on paid employment for women of her upbringing. She was also committing herself to a cause. She saw the end of lacemaking as an industry, but with a few fellow workers and pupils kept the craft alive in the 1930s and 1940s when it was at its lowest ebb. The lace collections at Luton Museum not only owe much to her generosity but have also been enriched by her expertise. My own debt to her for her interest and the insight she gave me into the history of the East Midlands lace industry is, I hope, obvious from what I have written here.

PLATE 14. Catherine C. Channer with pupil of one of the classes of the Bedford Technical Institute, held in a school classroom, 1925-30. *(Miss K. Richards)*

SELECT BIBLIOGRAPHY

Buck, A., *Thomas Lester, his Lace and the East Midlands Industry, 1820-1905*, Bedford 1981.

—— The teaching of lacemaking in the East Midlands, *Folk Life*, IV, 1966, pp. 39-50.

—— Middlemen in the Bedfordshire lace industry, *Beds Hist. Rec. Soc*, LVII, 1978, pp. 31-58.

Channer, C.C., *Practical Lacemaking, Bucks Point Ground*, Leicester 1928.

Cole, A.S., Report on the Northampton, Bucks. and Beds. Lacemaking, 1892.

Fitzrandolph, A.E., and Hay, M.D., *The Rural Industries of England and Wales, III*, Oxford 1927.

Freeman, C.E., *Pillow Lace in the East Midlands*, Luton 1958, rep. 1960.

Levey, S.M., *Lace, A History*, London 1983.

Palliser, Mrs Bury, *A History of Lace*, 4th rev. ed. by M. Jourdain and A. Dryden, 1902, rep. 1976.

Roberts, G.M., *Instructions in the Art of Making the Buckingham Pillow Lace*, Spratton, Northants 1926.

Spenceley, G.F.R., The Lace Associations: Philanthropic movements to preserve the production of hand-made lace in Late Victorian and Edwardian England, *Vict. Stud.*, XVI, 1973, pp. 433-52.

Wardle, P., *Victorian Lace*, 1968, 2nd ed., Bedford 1982.

Wright, T., *The Romance of the Lace Pillow*, 1919, 2nd ed., 1924, rep. Bedford 1982.

INDEX

* It was impractical to list individually the many types of lace mentioned in *Lace-making in the Midlands*.

Other Lace, Costume and Embroidery Books

Traditional Bedfordshire Lace - Technique and Patterns
Barbara M Underwood
0 903585 24 3   270 x 212, 100p, 200ill, folding sheet, hardbound

Bedfordshire Lace Patterns - A selection by Margaret Turner
0 903585 21 9   280 x 210mm, 112p 145ill, folding sheet, limpbound

Manual of Bedfordshire Lace Pamela Robinson
0 903585 20 0   247 x 233mm, 112p, 151ill, limpbound

Lace Flowers and How to Make Them Joyce Willmot
0 903585 23 5   187 x 156mm, 76p, 46pl & diagr incl colour, hardbound

The Technique & Design of Cluny Lace L Paulis/Maria Rutgers
0 903585 18 9   220 x 174, 96p, 130ill, hardbound

Victorian Costume & Costume Accessories Anne Buck
0 903585 17 0   220 x 174mm, 224p, 90ill, paperback

Le Pompe 1559 Santina Levey/Pat Payne
(Patterns for Venetian Bobbin Lace)
0 903585 16 2   243 x 177mm, 128p, 97ill, paperback

Teach Yourself Torchon Lace Eunice Arnold
0 903585 08 1   240 x 190mm, 40p, 6workcards, 27ill, limpbound

Pillow Lace - A Practical Hand-book E Mincoff/M Marriage
0 903585 10 3   216 x 138mm, 304p, 2worksheets, 90ill, hardbound

Victorian Lace Patricia Wardle
0 903585 13 8   222 x 141mm, 304p, 82pl, hardbound

Thomas Lester His Lace & E Midlands Industry 1820-1905 Anne Buck
0 903585 09 X   280 x 210mm, 120p, 55pl, hardbound

Tailor's Pattern Book 1589 Juan de Alcega
(Libro de Geometria, Pratica y Traça)
0 903585 06 5   279 × 203mm, 244p, 137ill, clothbound

Books on Textiles from:

RUTH BEAN Publishers

VICTORIA FARMHOUSE
CARLTON
BEDFORD MK43 7LP
ENGLAND